BL

Smart
SHELVING &
STORAGE
SOLUTIONS

Danny Proulx

POPULAR WOODWORKING BOOKS
CINCINNATI, OHIO
www.popularwoodworking.com

Disclaimer

To prevent accidents, keep safety in mind while you work. Use the safety guards installed on power equipment; they are for your protection. When working on power equipment, keep fingers away from saw blades, wear safety goggles to prevent injuries from flying wood chips and sawdust, wear headphones to protect your hearing, and consider installing a dust vacuum to reduce the amount of airborne sawdust in your woodshop. Don't wear loose clothing, such as neckties or shirts with loose sleeves, or jewelry, such as rings, necklaces or bracelets, when working on power equipment, and tie back long hair to prevent it from getting caught in your equipment. People who are sensitive to certain chemicals should check the chemical content of any product before using it. The author and editors who compiled this book have tried to make all the contents as accurate and correct as possible. Plans, illustrations, photographs and text have been carefully checked. All instructions, plans and projects should be carefully read, studied and understood before beginning construction. Due to the variability of local conditions, construction materials, skill levels, etc., neither the author nor *Popular Woodworking Books* assumes any responsibility for any accidents, injuries, damages or other losses incurred resulting from the material presented in this book.

METRIC CONVERSION CHART		
TO CONVERT	**TO**	**MULTIPLY BY**
Inches	Centimeters	2.54
Centimeters	Inches	0.4
Feet	Centimeters	30.5
Centimeters	Feet	0.03
Yards	Meters	0.9
Meters	Yards	1.1
Sq. Inches	Sq. Centimeters	6.45
Sq. Centimeters	Sq. Inches	0.16
Sq. Feet	Sq. Meters	0.09
Sq. Meters	Sq. Feet	10.8
Sq. Yards	Sq. Meters	0.8
Sq. Meters	Sq. Yards	1.2
Pounds	Kilograms	0.45
Kilograms	Pounds	2.2
Ounces	Grams	28.4
Grams	Ounces	0.04

Smart Shelving and Storage Solutions. Copyright © 1999 by Danny Proulx. Manufactured in the United States of America. All rights reserved. No part of this book may be reproduced in any form or by any electronic or mechanical means including information storage and retrieval systems without permission in writing from the publisher, except by a reviewer, who may quote brief passages in a review. Published by Popular Woodworking Books, an imprint of F&W Publications, Inc., 1507 Dana Avenue, Cincinnati, Ohio, 45207. First edition.

Other fine Popular Woodworking Books are available from your local bookstore or direct from the publisher.

Visit our Web site at www.popularwoodworking.com for information on more resources for woodworkers.

03   02   01   00   99   5   4   3   2   1

Library of Congress Cataloging in Publication Data

Proulx, Danny
    Smart shelving and storage solutions / Danny Proulx -- 1st ed.
        p.   cm.
    Includes index.
    ISBN 1-55870-509-0 (alk. paper)
    1. Cabinetwork Amateurs' manuals.   2. Shelving (Furniture)
    Amateurs' manuals.   3. Storage in the home Amateurs' manuals.
    I. Title.
    TT197.P76 1999   99-21730
    684.1'6--dc21   CIP

Edited by Bruce Stoker, Mark Thompson
Designed by Wendy Dunning
Cover designed by Brian Roeth
Production coordinated by Kristen Heller

Dedication

When I sit at the computer to type the dedication, I always think of the dozens of people who've contributed to my books. And I always worry about leaving someone out. To those that I have, my sincerest apologies—I have not forgotten you.

To my wife Gale, who is always there with helpful comments and assistance when needed. My father-in-law, Jack Chaters, has been my very able and willing assistant on each project. And to Michael Bowie whose photographic artistry makes my work look better than it is in reality, as well as Adam Blake and Bruce Stoker, my editors at Popular Woodworking Books. My deepest thanks to all of you who've helped make this book possible.

Acknowledgments

There have been many suppliers who have contributed products, material and technical support during the project building phase.

I appreciate how helpful they've been and recommend the companies without hesitation. They are listed in the back of this book in the "Sources" section.

About the Author

Danny Proulx has been involved in the woodworking field for more than 30 years. He has operated a custom kitchen cabinet shop since 1989.

He is a contributing editor to *CabinetMaker* magazine and has published articles in other magazines such as Canadian Workshop and WoodShop News.

His earlier books include *Build Your Own Kitchen Cabinets*, *The Kitchen Cabinetmaker's Building and Business Manual*, and *How to Build Classic Garden Furniture*.

His Web site address is http://www.cabinetmaking.com and he can be reached by email at danny@cabinetmaking.com.

TABLE OF CONTENTS

INTRODUCTION

It's been a long time coming. I've been promising myself that I'd get my home and shop organized someday. And, this book is the start of that someday.

My dear wife, Gale, has been suggesting in strong terms for a couple of years that we should complete some of the projects we've started. That bedroom project with a few pieces of furniture, and good intentions of finishing the remainder, has fallen by the wayside. Each time I walk by the unfinished rooms, I promise myself that I will complete the project next week.

When my editor at Popular Woodworking Books, Adam Blake, suggested a book about home storage projects, I jumped at the chance. Finally, I could organize my workshop and home with some really useful projects. Gale began by assigning the projects to specific rooms in the house like some sort of furniture shopping list. She directed projects to rooms saying, "this goes here, that goes there, and when will you be finished with this one." So much for selling the completed projects as I normally do after writing a woodworking book. I had my marching orders!

I decided to divide the book by areas. Instead of detailing thirty projects, one after the other, I dedicated each chapter to a room or area. Projects that seemed best suited to a particular room are contained in that chapter. But that doesn't mean you can't use a few of the suggested projects in other areas of your home. With the exception of putting a storage bed in your kitchen, most of the projects are easily applied to other rooms in your home. I've divided them in a general sense. However, you're the best judge of what will work for you.

My primary objective has been the creation of effective and ingenious storage projects. Practical, simple projects, that serve more than one function, and make the best possible use of space. More importantly though, I wanted to create storage furniture that looks good. It's easy to build a box to hold toys and stick it in a corner. But, it's an entirely different matter to build a nice looking box to hold toys that can be displayed as part of the room's furnishings. I believe we've accomplished our goals based on the comments from those that have seen the completed projects.

Most importantly, this book is not a vehicle to show how much I know about woodworking. I'm not a woodworking purest. Nor do I claim to know everything there is to know about this subject. I'm learning each day—even after thirty years of gluing sticks together. Hopefully, this book will stimulate other ways and means of working at wood. I've tried to offer one, simple alternative with each project.

Now it's time to really get organised and build some beautiful and unique home storage projects. I hope you have as much fun as I've had building these great woodworking projects.

OVERVIEW

Many people, myself included, don't make effective use of the available space in our homes. For example, our beds take up a good portion of the bedroom. We use that bed about thirty percent of the time and walk around it the remainder of the time. What about the unused space under, over and behind the bed? That's a lot of valuable real estate going to waste.

The Basics

We begin by looking at the basic structure of cabinets and shelving. They're nothing more than boxes— simple structures that serve a purpose. We are, as my cabinetmaker father often said, "just putting a few sticks together." It really is that simple.

Garage/Workshop

The first "room" in this book is the garage/workshop. Some of you have dedicated areas for each, while others have dual-purpose areas. Often, the garage serves as part workshop and part car park. Nevertheless, it's difficult to build projects for other rooms in your home when the workshop is unorganized.

Basement

I think many of us would call our basements the "catch-all." Anything that isn't used on a daily basis is often sent to the cellar. Even if you don't have the luxury or curse of a basement in your home, the projects in this chapter are easily adaptable to other rooms.

Laundry Room

Many laundry rooms suffer from a lack of work tables and storage cabinets. The tops of washers and dryers usually double as tables. It's a strange situation because this area desperately needs work surfaces and storage cabinets.

A base cabinet with doors and adjustable shelving would be a welcome addition to the laundry room. A rolltop or custom countertop can be attached for the work surface.

Wall cabinets are inexpensive and simple to build. You'll wonder why you hadn't tackled this project sooner. The storage space these cabinets provide is amazing.

Closet Storage

Closet spaces are unique, and each person has his or her own needs. I'll show you a system for a shared closet that you can modify to suit your needs. This is another simple project that helps organize your life.

Bathrooms

The "Vanity Base With Towers" project is an idea I picked up at a home show. What a great way to make the most effective use of space in this small room! There is storage for towels, bath products and all the personal products that are commonly found in modern bathrooms.

Living Areas

Most of the "living" rooms in the home, like bedrooms, family rooms and kitchen areas, are ideal candidates for improved storage furniture.

I'll show you how to build a couple of entertainment units and a bookcase for the family room. The best rooms to tackle, however, are the bedrooms. There are dozens of project possibilities for these areas. I'll detail some of the best I've seen.

The Projects

You'll find over twenty-five dynamic and unique storage projects. Most of them are constructed using simple joinery methods. Remember that your goal is to improve home storage and keep it simple.

Basic Cabinet and Shelf Construction

Many of the projects in this book include some form of basic cabinetry or shelving. This chapter explains cabinet and shelving construction principles that will be useful when you begin building your project.

CABINETRY

Cabinet Terminology

There are specific names identifying cabinet parts used throughout this book. These names clearly describe the various parts of a cabinet and are widely used in the industry.

There are two basic types of kitchen and bathroom cabinets—frameless and face frame. The front edges of the top, bottom and sides of the frameless style are exposed and covered with edge tape. The traditional North American face-frame cabinet has a wood frame attached to the front edges of the cabinet body.

An upper- or wall-cabinet carcass is made up of five pieces, two sides, a back, top and bottom. The standard base is constructed with two sides, a back and a bottom. The base units have adjustable legs or base platforms and don't require a top because the counter sits on the cabinet.

The European-style hidden hinge is a popular cabinet door hinge.

The Hidden Hinge

The hidden or European hinge will be used on many projects. The design of this hinge allows for very accurate placement of the cabinet doors because of the hinge's mechanical ability to hold that placement. The European hinge was developed on European-style cabinetry or cabinets without the traditional North American face frame. However, the European hinge is widely used on face-frame cabinets as well.

A full-overlay European hinge is meant to fully cover or overlay the front side edge of the cabinet. Carcass thickness is normally ⅝", so a full-overlay European hinge covers approximately ⅝" of the cabinet face.

Hinges are classified by degrees of opening. A 90° hinge will allow the door to swing fully open at a right angle to the cabinet face edge. There are many opening capacities available, but I use a 120° hinge for the majority of situations. As you will see, the flexibility of these hinges is impressive and installation is easy.

Adjustable base cabinet legs simplify installation.

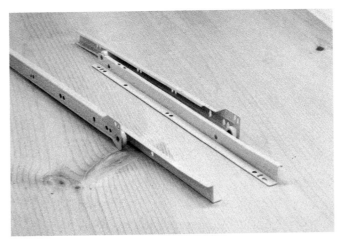

European-style drawer glides eliminate wood support framing. The drawers slide effortlessly on nylon rollers.

Adjustable Base Legs

Adjustable cabinet legs will be used on some of the projects. In base cabinets without legs, the sides are longer, or a base frame is built to provide the under-cabinet clearance called the toe-kick space.

These adjustable legs are a great alternative and save time when installing the cabinet. Where water on the floor is a possibility, such as in the laundry room, cabinet legs will be used.

Drawer Glides

Another dramatic departure from the traditional North American style of cabinetry is the use of European drawer glides.

These glides consist of two drawer runners and two side runners. You don't have to build hardwood drawer rails and inset drawer bottoms, which increases the design possibilities. In some of these projects we'll use a 75-pound rated bottom-mounted drawer glide. Build the drawer body using the same method as an upper-cabinet carcass. Building drawers will be detailed in a later chapter.

STORAGE CABINETRY

Storage cabinets are built in the same fashion as kitchen cabinets and can be made from almost any type of sheet goods. For the garage you may want to use inexpensive plywood or particleboard. For the family room it may be more suitable to use a veneer-covered plywood or particleboard. No matter the material, there are a few simple rules to grasp.

Base and upper cabinets are simple to build once you understand the component size relationship. The width, height and depth relate to each other and determine the door size.

It doesn't matter whether you prefer a European frameless cabinet or a more traditional North American face-frame cabinet, the door, or combined width of two doors, is 1" wider than the bottom board. We'll follow this rule throughout the book using ⅝"- and ¹¹⁄₁₆"-thick sheet goods as our standards.

Melamine-coated particleboard cabinets are simple to build. The melamine is available in many colors.

of each component for a 24"-wide frameless wall cabinet.

There are a few assumptions I've made when building these cabinets. First, the material is ⅝" thick. Second, we are using the European hidden, full-overlay hinge to mount the doors. And third, the doors are made from the same ⅝"-thick material with taped edges. Take edge-tape thickness into account when cutting the doors.

Wall-mounted upper cabinets are built with five boards as earlier detailed: two sides, a top, bottom and one back. My preference is to use ⅝"-thick material for the back, when practical, which results in a very strong cabinet. See the Helping Hand section on page 14 for proper procedures for hanging wall cabinets. There are, however, instances when a ¼" back board can be used.

For the upper cabinets in the workshop, garage and laundry rooms, the doors will be made from the same material as the carcass. When building more formal cabinets, such as for the family room or bedroom, we will probably want to cover the sides and bottoms with veneer and use fancy wood doors.

Materials List

No.	Item	Dimensions T W L
2	Sides	⅝"x11½"x31"
1	Top	⅝"x11½"x22¾"
1	Bottom	⅝"x11½"x22¾"
1	Back	⅝"x24"x31"
2	Doors	⅝"x11⅞"x31"
1	Shelves	⅝"x11½"x22⅝"

I'll build most of the doors for these projects. However, you may want to purchase ready-made raised-panel wood doors for the more involved projects rather than investing in expensive router bits.

Frameless Wall Cabinets

As shown above, melamine-coated particleboard is available in a variety of colors. It has a finished surface, so a color-matched cabinet can be ready for your room in no time.

As I will illustrate during the many projects where melamine particleboard is used, hardware and the proper installation of that joinery hardware is critical.

The materials list details the size

Frameless Base Cabinets

Base cabinets differ from upper cabinets because they require a support structure, which can be legs or a wood base. They are built without a top board because a countertop or cabinet top often serves that purpose.

For the most part, we will use a full-thickness back on these cabinets to provide strength and rigidity. We depend on material thickness and fastening devices for strength when using particleboard sheet goods because most glues don't bond well to the coated surfaces.

Hardware and Joinery

The basic construction goal of these designs is a very strong carcass, or box, as the body for each modular cabinet or shelf system. The ⅝" particleboard is butt jointed and secured with special screws every 4". If you can find them, use MDF or particleboard screws. Otherwise, use drywall screws with deep, sharp threads.

Wood face frames are constructed using butt joints, glue and two wood screws at each joint. Other joining options include biscuits, pocket screws on the rear of the face frame, or a mortise-and-tenon joint. This wood face frame is then attached to the carcass front using glue and 2" spiral finishing nails.

Nails are countersunk, and the holes are covered with colored wood filler wax, making them nearly invisible. Use biscuits to avoid nailing and filling. Under normal circumstances, the closed cabinet door will cover the filled nail holes.

SHELVING

Shelving follows the same basic principles as cabinet construction. We want to use the correct material with solid mechanical joints. Glue and screws or nails will be used in conjunction with standard joinery principles.

Where possible, shelf units should be adjustable to provide maximum efficiency. In some cases that means a little extra material and labor, but adjustable shelves really do make a difference in the flexibility of your projects.

Shelf Construction

We'll discuss different shelving options with specific projects, but some concepts should be kept in mind when building shelving units.

Most storage shelves tend to be loaded with all sorts of heavy items. Shelving in the family room or bedroom often contains books. It is therefore important to build shelf systems that are capable of supporting heavy objects. We sometimes assume a particular shelf will only contain towels, for instance, but situations change. That shelf might be used to store cleaning products. The shelving projects in this book will be built to take as much weight as possible.

There are many types of adjustable support systems for shelves, such as the metal pin assembly. Another popular adjustable shelf system, called a standard, uses a metal pilaster and metal clip.

Fancy adjustable shelf pins are available for more formal bookcases, such as those in a library. They are supplied with a brass tube that is inserted into a hole with a special punch. The shelf pin sits in the brass tube and is a piece of hardware meant to complement the expensive woods that are often used.

The goal for most of the shelf projects in this book is to design and build a unit that's strong. Joinery, glue and mechanical fasteners will support the weight these shelves will be certain to carry. Who knows, one of your children may decide their new bookcase makes a great ladder or jungle gym!

Plastic-covered metal pins are a popular adjustable shelf-support application.

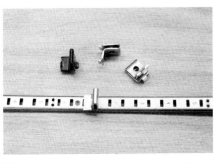

The commonly used metal pilaster and clip system can support a lot of weight.

Fancy solid-brass shelf-support brackets are used for "high end"-type shelving and cabinetry.

Skill Builder Building a Typical Base Cabinet

Before we get into the first project, I want to describe the common method of building a cabinet. First and foremost, cut all parts as accurately as possible. A little extra effort at this stage of the project will pay big dividends when you begin the assembly process.

Step 1. Cut the Parts

Accurately cut all parts for the cabinet prior to assembly.

Step 2. Attach the Legs

If you plan on using the adjustable leg system, drill a hole for each leg bolt so the leg flange hangs over the base board edge by about ½". The legs I'm using require the bolt holes to be ⅝" on center from the edge.

By installing the legs in this manner, we are assured that the edge of the gable end or cabinet side will rest on the leg flange, transferring the cabinet load to the floor. Install the legs, but don't fully tighten them at this point.

Step 3. Drill the Adjustable Shelf Holes

Each side (gable end) will require two rows of holes for adjustable shelves on the inside surface. These can be laid out with a ruler, or a simple jig can be built as shown in the Helping Hand procedure on page 26 in chapter two.

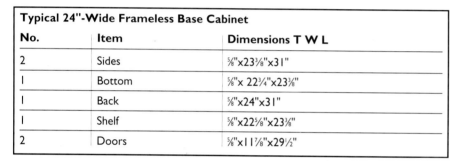

No.	Item	Dimensions T W L
Typical 24"-Wide Frameless Base Cabinet		
2	Sides	⅝"x23⅜"x31"
1	Bottom	⅝"x 22¾"x23⅜"
1	Back	⅝"x24"x31"
1	Shelf	⅝"x22⅝"x23⅜"
2	Doors	⅝"x11⅞"x29½"

Step 1. Accurately cutting all parts will pay off in the assembly stage.

Step 2. Install the adjustable base legs.

Step 3. Hole spacing for adjustable shelving is normally 2" or less.

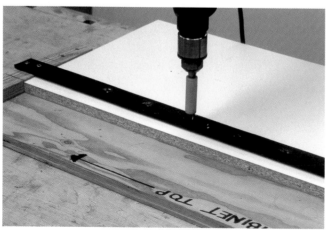

Step 4. The cabinet sides are attached flush with the bottom of the base board edge using 2" particleboard, MDF or drywall screws.

Step 4. Attach the Sides

Be certain to predrill and counter-sink the holes before inserting the screws. This insures that the screw will cut a thread in the board rather than splitting the material. Install screws approximately 4" apart. After securing both sides with screws, tighten the cabinet legs.

Step 5. Install the Back Board

Cutting the back board accurately insures the cabinet will be square when it's attached. Predrill the screw holes, and insert the screws about 4" apart.

Step 6. Install the Countertop Brackets

Step 7. Attach the Top Rail

Attach a top rail on base cabinets so the doors can be installed 1½" below the cabinet's top edge. This will allow the doors to clear the overhang of the countertop. Normally this board is 2" high and as wide as the base board. It is installed flush with the top edge of each cabinet side.

To complete the base cabinet, see chapter four, page 45, "Building Cabinet Doors" and chapter four, page 52, "Installing Cabinet Doors With Hidden Hinges."

That's basically all there is to building a frameless-style base cabinet. A face-frame or traditional cabinet follows the same procedures with the exception of an added wood face frame that is attached to the cabinet's front edges.

PRO TIP

After ripping the boards, I usually apply the edge tape and let the saw cut the ends cleanly.

Step 5. Attach the cabinet back with 2" screws.

Step 6. Install two brackets on each side and two on the back board with ⅝" particleboard, MDF or drywall screws. Make sure the clips are flush with the top of each edge.

Step 7. Installing a base cabinet top rail.

⚒ *Helping Hand*   Hanging Wall Cabinets

Step 1. Locate the Wall Studs

There are a number of methods used to determine the stud location in a wall. You can tap the wall gently, listening for a sound change, or look for evidence of drywall screws. However, the easiest method is to use a stud locator.

Step 2. Find Stud Spacing

Measure to the right and left of that stud to determine stud spacing. Normally they are spaced at 16" or 24".

Step 3. Mark the Stud Lines

Using a long level, mark the stud lines. If you don't want to mark the wall, use masking tape.

Step 4. Level the Cabinet

Place the cabinet against the wall. It can be temporarily supported with a strap screwed to the wall or by a deadman. See chapter four, page

Step 1. Locating studs with an electronic finder.

Step 2. Determine the stud spacing.

Step 3. Extend the stud location lines above and below the cabinet space.

PRO TIP

Cabinets can be raised or lowered, as well as plumbed, by using tapered cedar shim stock to correct any errors. Always place the shim as close as possible to the cabinet anchor screws.

46, for instructions on how to build a deadman.

Step 5. Secure the Cabinet

Once the cabinet is placed correctly, predrill a hole through the cabinet back and into the wall stud. Secure the cabinet through the back board with a 3" screw.

Step 6. Verify Placement

Before installing the remainder of the screws, verify that the cabinet is correctly positioned. As a general rule, I use four screws per cabinet up to 30" wide.

Step 7. Final Checks

After the cabinet is securely anchored, check that it's level and plumb to ensure it didn't move or twist when the screws were installed.

Step 8. Join Common Cabinets

If two frameless cabinets—either wall or base units—are side by side, they can be attached to each other.

Step 5. Attach the cabinet with 3" screws.

Step 7. Always double-check the cabinet after installing the wall anchors.

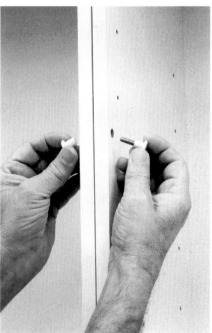

Step 8. Adjoining cabinets can be secured to each other with cap screws.

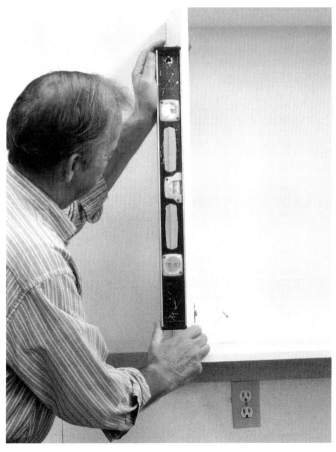

PRO TIP

How many screws do you need to properly attach a wall cabinet? That depends on many factors. How is the cabinet constructed? Is the material thick and strong? What will the cabinet contain? Dishware can be heavy while paper products and linen are relatively light. Analyze the load and use for each application. As a general rule, err on the side of caution. As the saying goes, "better one nail too many than one too few."

Garage and Woodshop Storage

Mobile Work Center

The mobile work center has proven to be a useful addition to my shop. When I'm in the garage, it serves as a workbench and tool holder. In the shop, I use it for my planer and small drill press. I've also found it handy near the miter saw when I have a lot of small pieces to cut.

BUILDING THE WORKBENCH

Step 1. Cut the Carcass Parts
Accurately cut all the pieces for the cabinet box.

Step 2. Prepare the Pieces
Sand all the outside front edges of the base board and sides prior to assembly.

Step 3. Attach the Sides
Connect the sides to the base board using 2" screws and glue. Predrill

Step 3. Join the sides of the base board with glue and 2" wood screws.

Step 4. Install the back board with 2" screws at 6" centers.

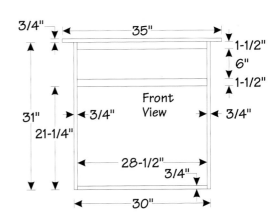

Front view of workbench carcass.

Step 5. Use two 2" screws per side to attach the crosspieces (rails).

Step 6. Corner blocks are installed to add strength to the cabinet. They also anchor the top.

Materials List

All pieces are cut from ¾" Good One Side plywood.

No.	Item	Dimensions T W L
2	Sides	¾"x22"x31"
1	Base	¾"x22"x28½"
1	Back	¾"x30"x31"
1	Top	¾"x25"x35"
2	Rails	¾"x1½"x28½"

> ### PRO TIP
>
> Remember, if the back board is cut square, it will square the cabinet. Take the time to ensure an accurate cut.

the holes before inserting screws. Space screws at approximately 6" centers.

Step 4. Install the Back Board

Install the back board with screws and glue. Always predrill the screw holes for maximum hold.

Step 5. Install the Rails

Attach the two front crosspieces with glue and 2" screws. Space the pieces as shown in drawing above.

Step 6. Attach the Corner Blocks

With blocks cut from a 2x4 at a 45° angle, reinforce the top corners.

Step 7. Install Wheel Pads

The bottom corners have ¾"-thick by 3"-square blocks. They will add strength to the bottom and allow wheels to be securely attached.

Step 8. Install Base Wheels

I'm using a 4"-high, 3"-diameter wheel assembly that can be locked.

Step 7. Pads are attached with glue and screws to support cabinet wheels. Apply glue, and use three 1¼" screws per pad.

Step 8. Industrial-grade wheel assemblies with locks are installed at the corners of the cabinet.

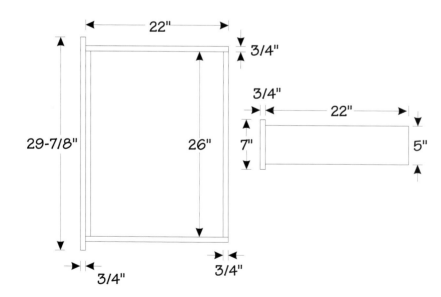

Drawer box construction details.

The lock feature is important when a planer or drill press is mounted on the table. Use ⁵⁄₁₆"x1¼"-long lag bolts to secure the wheels.

Step 9. Build the Drawer

The drawer is a simple "box" made from ¾" plywood. I am using bottom-mounted drawer glides, so the box must be 1" narrower and 1" lower than the drawer opening. Construct the drawer box, as shown in the drawing below, using glue and 2" screws.

Step 10. Complete the Drawer Box

Sand the top edges of the plywood drawer box. Round over the inner and outer top edges of the box with a ¼" router bit.

Step 11. Install the Drawer Glides

Using 22" bottom-mounted drawer glides, install as per the manufacturer's instructions.

Step 12. Cut the Drawer Face

The overlay drawer face is simply another piece of ¾" plywood, 7"-high by 29⅞"-wide. The good side is face out, and the edges are sanded and rounded over with a router bit.

Step 13. Install the Top

The top board's edges are sanded and rounded over. I've also used a belt sander to ease the corners on the top to prevent injury should someone bump into the cabinet.

Step 9. Building the drawer box.

Step 10. Sand the drawer and round over both inner and outer edges to prevent splinters.

Step 11. Bottom-mounted, or Euro-style, drawer glides are the simplest and least expensive drawer-mounting system. Most glide sets are rated for a 75-pound capacity load.

PRO TIP

If you are concerned about installing screws in a ¾" butt joint, use a square set to ⅜", and mark a guideline for screw placement.

Step 12. Attach the drawer face with four 1¼" screws from inside the drawer box.

Step 13. Secure the top with a 2" screw through the corner support block at each corner.

Step 14. Attach the shelf to the sides using cleats. This approach allows you to customize the shelves you need.

Step 14. Add a Shelf

For this application, I've installed a three-quarter depth shelf. Cleats are attached to the side boards and the shelf is anchored through the cleats.

Step 15. Cut the Doors

Cut and attach two doors, each measuring ¾"x14¾"x22½". Mount 120° hidden hinges. Install the doors as detailed in chapter four, page 52.

Step 16. Paint the Work Center

The cabinet is now ready for finishing. For this project, I used two coats of oil-based white paint.

Step 15. Install hidden hinges and mount the cabinet doors.

The completed cabinet is ready for final sanding and finishing.

Workshop Base Cabinet

One corner of my workshop suffers from terminal clutter. Installing base cabinets with adjustable shelving should clean up a lot of the mess. This area really needs help!

I have enough space to install five linear feet of base cabinets. I've opted for two cabinets, one 24" wide and the other 36" wide.

I'll also show you how to build a low-cost laminated top for the base units. High-pressure laminate material is available in 60"-wide by 144"-long sheets so you can build 24' of 26"-deep countertops from one sheet.

Build the base cabinets as detailed in chapter one. I suggest you limit each base cabinet width to a maximum of 36" because door and shelving strengths decrease over wide spans.

Calculating the cut sizes for frameless cabinetry is not too difficult if you remember a few guidelines.

The sides for all sizes of cabinets are 23⅜"-wide by 31"-tall. The bottom board is as deep as the sides and 1¼" less than the cabinet width. For example, a 24"-wide cabinet would need a 23⅜"-deep bottom board that is 22¾" wide.

The back board is equal in size to the cabinet's finished width and side board height. The back board, then, is 24"-wide by 31"-tall.

The door, or doors in the case of a two-door cabinet, is 1" wider than the bottom board. When you install a 2"-high top rail, the door height is 1½" less than the cabinet side board, or 29½".

Step 1. Use 1¼" screws to join the cabinets.

Follow these simple guidelines and it's a simple matter to calculate all the part sizes for any size frameless cabinet.

Step 1. Join the Cabinets

Install the base units, making sure they are level and plumb, with the front edges of both flush to each other. Use 1¼" screws to tie the cabinets together.

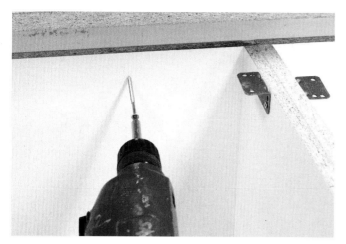

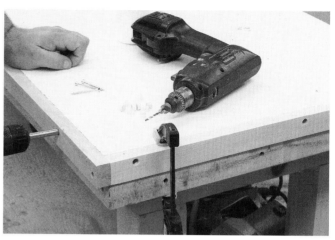

Step 2. Use a minimum of two 3" screws to attach the cabinets to the wall.

Step 3. Attach a wood edge to the countertop board.

PRO TIP

The effect when two pieces of wood are not drawn tightly together is called "bridging." The screw threads into both boards, causing a gap between them. To avoid bridging, drill a hole in the board on the screw head side. The hole should be a little larger than the screw-thread diameter. This will allow the screw to rotate freely, drawing the two boards tightly together.

Step 2. Attach the Cabinets to the Wall

Double-check that the cabinets are level as well as plumb. These cabinets are built with a full ⅝"-thick back, so you can place a screw anywhere in the back when attaching them to a wall stud.

BUILDING THE COUNTERTOP

One of my reasons for including this project is to detail an inexpensive method of building a high-quality countertop.

This style of top can be used anywhere a high-quality work surface is required. In fact, this style of countertop is widely used by kitchen cabinetmaking professionals.

Step 4. Prepare the top for the laminate by sanding the materials flush with each other.

Step 5. Trim the laminate flush with the countertop edge.

Step 6. Use a ⅜" router bit to form a decorative edge on the countertop.

Step 7. Test the router bit's depth so that the cut is only as deep as the laminate thickness.

Step 3. Prepare the Substrate

Any good ⅝" or ¾" plywood, particle- or high-density board can be used for the countertop substrate. Cut the material to ⅝"x25"x62".

Attach a wood edge flush with the substrate's top surface. Use glue and 2" screws in a counterbored hole that can be filled with a wood plug. In this application, I used ¾"-thick by 1½"-tall birch hardwood for the edge.

Step 4. Prepare the Top

Make certain the top surface of the wood edge is flush with the sheet material. If necessary, use a sander to even out the materials.

Step 5. Glue the Laminate

Cut the laminate material 2" wider and longer than the countertop substrate. Apply contact cement to both surfaces, and carefully place the laminate. Roll the material from the center to the outside. Once the laminate is securely attached, trim the overhang with a flush trim router bit.

Step 6. Rout the Wood Edge

On the edge of the countertop with the wood banding, cut the laminate and wood edge with a ⅜" roundover bit.

Step 7. Attach the Countertop

Round over the bottom of the wood edge. Note that the router depth is adjusted because you do not have to cut through a laminate thickness. Secure the countertop to the base cabinets with ⅝" screws through the metal right-angle brackets and into the countertop substrate.

Wall-Mounted Frameless Storage Cabinets

The frameless wall cabinet is a great, low-cost storage unit for the shop or garage. For that matter, this cabinet style is a great storage solution for any room in the home. I will use this cabinet to store small parts in my workshop. I'll use a form of this cabinet for a few projects throughout this book.

In chapter one, I discussed frameless wall cabinets. The example given was a two-door 24" cabinet, but a one-door 24" cabinet, like this one, is a typical application.

Step 1. Dress the Edges
Apply white edge tape to the exposed front edges of the cabinet sides, top and bottom. Apply the tape after ripping and prior to crosscutting to size. Now, as the boards are crosscut, the saw blade cuts the edge tape clean and square. Trim the excess tape off the edges with a knife or double edge trimmer.

Step 2. Drill Adjustable Shelf Holes
Drill holes for the adjustable shelves. These are normally spaced about 2" apart and can be laid out with a ruler. To make an inexpensive hole jig, see this chapter's Helping Hand on page 26.

Step 3. Attach the Sides
Secure the sides to the top and bottom boards. Use 2" particleboard, MDF or drywall screws in predrilled holes for maximum hold. Three screws per side are required.

Step 4. Install the Back Board
Secure the back with 2" screws installed at 8" spacing.

Step 5. Set the Shelf Pins
Use the adjustable shelf pins you prefer and set them in place.

Step 6. Hang the Cabinet
Attach the cabinet to the wall, as detailed in chapter one, page 14.

Step 7. Install the Cabinet Door
Refer to chapter four, page 52, for details on door installation.

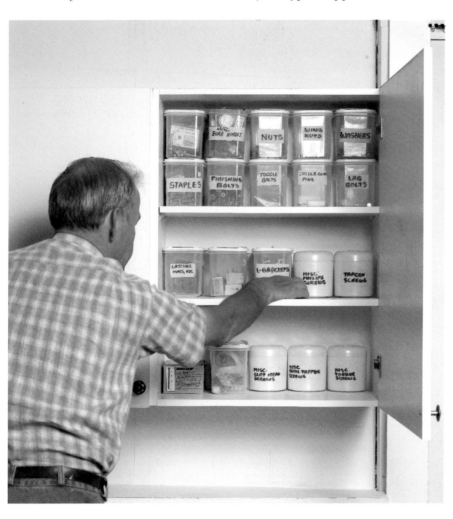

Materials List

Lay out and cut the pieces required for a 24" single-door wall cabinet. Use the following measurements.

No.	Item	Dimensions T W L
2	Sides	⅝"x12"x31"
1	Top	⅝"x12"x22¾"
1	Bottom	⅝"x12"x22¾"
1	Back	⅝"x24"x31"
2	Shelves	⅝"x12"x22⅝"
1	Door	⅝"x23¾"x31"

Step 2. Drill the necessary holes for adjustable shelves prior to assembling the cabinet.

Step 1. For best results, trim the edge tape with a low-cost double-sided tape trimmer.

Step 4. Install the back board with 2" screws. If the back board was cut square, the cabinet will be square.

Step 3. Attach the sides to the top and bottom boards.

 PRO TIP

Don't assume material thickness is standard, particularly with sheet goods such as particleboard. Different manufacturers use different measurement standards. Production runs, as well as humidity, can affect board thickness.

Step 5. Place the adjustable shelf pins in their correct positions.

⚒ *Helping Hand*   Building a Shelf Hole Jig

This jig is a handy shop tool. It will act as a guide for drilling accurately placed holes in cabinet sides up to 31" long. The flat steel is available at most hardware stores. All other materials are readily available from any home store.

Step 1. Cut the Platform

Cut a ¾"x13"x34¹⁄₁₆" piece of plywood.

Step 2. Attach the Bar Supports

Cut and attach two boards that are ¾"x1½"x10". Use four 1¼" screws per board. Install the boards flush at each end with 31¹⁄₁₆" between them.

Step 3. Label the Jig

To help keep the cabinet sides oriented properly, mark the jig as shown. When drilling shelf holes, I note the top of the cabinet side with an "X" on the edge of each board.

Step 4. Drill the Flat Steel

Prepare a piece of ¼"-thick flat steel 1½"-wide by 34"-long. Drill holes at 2" on center up the middle of the bar. If you prefer, you can increase or decrease the hole spacing.

    Decide which shelf pin you'll be using most often. Drill the guide holes to the diameter required for those pins. Locate two holes at either end of the flat steel, and attach it to the end boards with 1½" screws.

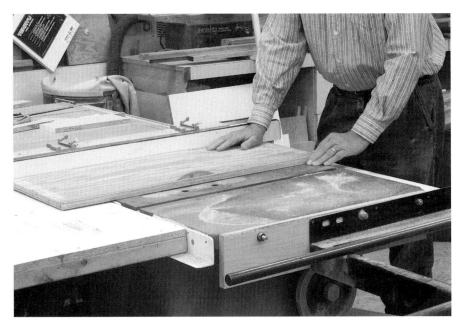

Step 1. Accurately cut a plywood platform for the jig.

Step 2. Secure the boards at each end with 1¼" screws.

Step 3. Label the jig to help you maintain correct side alignment when drilling cabinet sides.

Step 4. Drill and mount the guide bar.

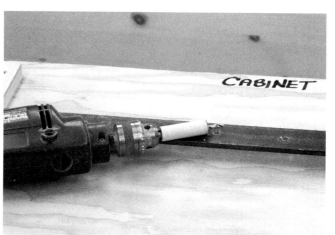

Step 5. Verify that all dimensions are correct on your shelf hole jig.

Step 6. Make a drill stop gauge using a dowel rod.

Step 5. Verify Measurements

The jig will accept cabinet sides up to ¾"-thick by 31"-long. If you want to drill shorter sides, put spacers in the jig to hold the cabinet side tight against the top board. Drill one vertical set of holes, and move the cabinet side over to drill the other set. Each cabinet side will require two parallel sets of holes. Guide marks on the jig's end boards will help position the holes 1" from each side board's edge.

Step 6. Make a Drill Stop

Drilling through a piece of dowel rod can make a simple drill-depth stop. Set the drill bit in the chuck with the stop in place, so the bit can travel through the steel and approximately three-quarters of the way through a cabinet side—deep enough that the shelf pin will be properly seated and secure. The stop will prevent the drill bit from exiting the finished face of the cabinet side.

Basement Storage

Aromatic Cedar Wardrobe

Aromatic red cedar is often used in clothes storage trunks and closets. It has a natural beauty and is prized for its ability to keep insects out. If you have seasonal clothes that must be stored in a clean, well-protected, dust-free area, then this is the project for you.

This type of cedar can be costly, but the sheet version, which uses the same process as chipboard manufacturing, is considerably cheaper. In my area, a 4'x8' sheet of aromatic cedar sells for under $30. This beautiful storage wardrobe can be built without the cedar lining.

BUILDING THE WARDROBE

Step 1. Cut the MDF Pieces
Important! Minimize waste by crosscutting the top and bottom panels from the 4'x8' MDF sheets before ripping the sides and back. By following this procedure you will only need two sheets of $^{11}/_{16}$" MDF.

Step 2. Attach the Sides
Connect the sides to the top and bottom boards with glue and 2" wood screws in predrilled holes.

Step 3. Install the Back Board
Attach the back board with yellow carpenter's glue and 2" screws. Cut the back board accurately, so the cabinet will be square. Space the screws about 6" apart.

Step 4. Install the Cabinet Legs
I am using plastic, adjustable cabinet legs for my application because the wardrobe will reside in my basement where there is a possibility of water leakage. If you plan on keeping this wardrobe in a more formal setting, a good option is to build a birch base from 1"x4" stock.

Step 1. Crosscut the top and bottom MDF panels before ripping the sides and back panels.

Step 2. Attach the cabinet sides to the top and bottom boards with glue and screws.

Step 3. Attach the back board with glue and 2" screws.

Step 4. Install the cabinet legs.

Secure the legs as per the manufacturer's recommendations. Install two on each side and two in the center. Attach the outside legs so their flange is covering the side-panel ends. This will transfer the load from the side and bottom panels to the floor.

Step 5. Covering the MDF Top and Sides

You can either paint the exterior surface of the cabinet or cover the sides and top with ¼" veneer plywood. Any wood can be used for the exterior panels. If you like the look of red oak or mahogany, substitute it for the birch veneer and hardwood.

Materials List

This project is built with medium-density fiberboard (MDF), birch veneer plywood (BVP) and aromatic cedar sheets (ARC). The face frame is made of birch hardwood.

No.	Item	Dimensions T W L	Materials
2	Sides	¹¹/₁₆"x23"x72"	MDF
1	Top	¹¹/₁₆"x23"x46¼"	MDF
1	Bottom	¹¹/₁₆"x23"x46¼"	MDF
1	Back	¹¹/₁₆"x47⅝"x72"	MDF
2	Sides	¼"x23¹¹/₁₆"x72¼"	BVP
1	Top	¼"x23¹¹/₁₆"x47⅝"	BVP
2	Stiles	¾"x1½"x72¾"	Birch
1	Bottom rail	¾"x1½"x45⅛"	Birch
1	Top rail	¾"x2"x45⅛"	Birch
1	Center stile	¾"x1½"x69¼"	Birch
1	Support	¾"x2½"x70"	Birch
3	Sheets	³/₁₆"x4'x8'	ARC
4	Door panels	¼"x19½"x33⅛"	BVP
6	Door stiles	¾"x1½"x69⅛"	Birch
6	Door rails	¾"x1½"x19⅝"	Birch

Step 5. Install the veneer top and side panels with panel adhesive and brad nails.

Step 6. Install the aromatic cedar panels on the cabinet interior surfaces.

Step 7. When you install the cabinet stiles, be sure to drill a countersink for the nail's head.

Step 8. Install the bottom rail.

Apply the veneer to the top, then to the sides, so the side panels will cover the edges of the top panel. Use construction or panel adhesive, as well as a few brad nails, to hold the panel in place until the cement sets.

Step 6. Attach the Aromatic Cedar Panels

Cut the aromatic red cedar sheets so they cover the inside back, sides, top and bottom of the cabinet. Use panel adhesive and brad nails to secure the panels.

BUILDING THE FACE FRAME

Step 7. Attach the Stiles

Cut two birch hardwood stiles to ¾"x1½"x72¾". Secure them to the cabinet's outer edges with glue and 2" spiral finishing nails through the face and into the MDF edge. Fill the countersunk nail holes with matching wood putty.

The stiles are installed flush with the outer side of the cabinet. The tops of the stiles are even with the cabinet's top surface and hang ½" below the bottom board.

Step 8. Install the Bottom Rail

Cut the bottom rail to ¾"x1½"x45⅛". Install so it's even with the aromatic cedar sheet on the bottom of the cabinet. Use glue and 2" spiral finishing nails (space about 6" apart).

Step 9. Attach the Top Rail

The top rail is ¾"x2"x45⅛" and is attached in the same manner as the bottom rail. Its top edge is flush with the stiles, and its bottom edge extends into the cabinet space.

Step 9. Cut and install the top rail.

Step 10. Fasten the Center Stile

Cut a center stile to ¾"x1½"x69¼" and attach. Secure it with glue and a 3" screw through the top rail. Attach the bottom with glue and a 2" screw through the bottom rail. Both screws will thread into the ends of the center rail, holding it while the glue sets up. To strengthen the butt joints, attach a center stile support and doorstop board. Be certain that the center stile is equally spaced between both outside stiles. This is critical for proper inset door fitting and operation.

Step 10. Secure the center stile with glue and screws through the top and bottom rails.

Step 11. Install the Center Support/Doorstop

The doorstop board is ¾"x2½"x70". It is placed directly behind the center stile. This board overlaps the backsides of the top and bottom rails. Use glue with 1¼" screws from the rear, in pilot holes, to secure the doorstop to the rails and center stile. There should be a ½" edge formed on each side of the center stile. This edge will ensure that the door closes flush with the center stile face.

 **PRO TIP**

My center stile board had a slight bow. This would affect the proper operation of the doors, but the center stile support and doorstop act as a "strong back" for the center stile, so a slight adjustment is possible. Measure the center stile to outside stile distance. If it isn't equal from top to bottom, move the center stile to correct the error, and clamp it against the support board. Glue and screw both boards to each other from the rear side.

Step 12. Sand and round over the outside edges of the face frame.

Step 13. Cut the door-frame stiles and rails. Form dadoes and tenons as detailed.

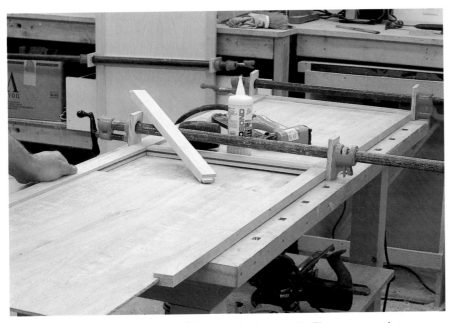

Step 14. Build the door frame using ¾" hardwood stiles and rails. The center panels are ¼" veneer plywood.

Step 12. Dress the Outside Edges

Sand the face-frame members, and round over the outside edges of the stiles and rails with a ¼" roundover bit.

BUILDING THE DOORS

The doors have an outside measurement of 21⅝"-wide by 69⅛"-long for my cabinet. Check the opening dimensions on your cabinet in case there are slight variances. Begin by building the door ⅛" smaller than the width and height of the opening.

Step 13. Cut the Door Stiles and Rails

Cut the stiles and rails as shown in the materials list. Then, using a dado blade on the table saw, or a ¼" bit on a router table, form a ¼"-wide by ½"-deep dado on one edge of all the frame pieces. The two center rails need a dado on both long edges to accept the ¼" center panel. Additionally, form a tenon that's ½"-long by ¼"-thick on both ends of the six rails.

Step 14. Prepare the Door Panels

Cut four pieces of veneer plywood to ¼"x19½"x33⅛" for the door center panels. The panels are slightly undersized to allow for movement.

As always, verify your panel measurements by dry fitting the door-frame members. Assemble the doors by securing one end rail and the two stiles. Use glue on the tenons and a brad nail through the stile and tenon on the rear of the door. Insert the first plywood panel, then a center rail, the next panel and finally the last end rail.

Step 15. Install the Interior Door Panels

Install a ³⁄₁₆" aromatic cedar panel to the back side of each door. The panel height is the same as the door, and the width is shortened by ⅝", so the door will close tightly.

Step 15. Attach the interior cedar door panels.

Step 17. Install the doorlatch system.

Step 16. Fit the Doors

Lay the cabinet on its back, and test fit the doors. It may be necessary to sand or plane to achieve a perfect fit. Use shims to hold the door in position while installing the hinges.

There are many hinge options available, so choose one that suits your application. A more formal setting than a basement may require hinge systems such as a piano hinge or a mortised butt hinge. I chose to use 3" butt hinges, which are simply attached on the exterior surface of the doors.

Step 17. Install the Door Lock

Once again, the area where the cabinet will be placed, as well as the number of times the cabinet will be used, will be what determines the door-closing hardware. My application is simply long-term storage, so a hardwood block, pivoting on a screw, is suitable. You might want a handle-and-latch mechanism if the cabinet will be used on a daily basis.

Step 18. Fit the Interior Shelves

There are many options for interior shelving. The decision depends on the type of material that will be

stored. The majority of my storage will be coats, so a simple wire rack is a perfect choice. I found an inexpensive 12"-deep plastic-coated metal rack. Originally 48" long, I cut the rack to fit and secured it to the cabinet with clips that were included with the rack.

Step 19. Sand and Finish the Wardrobe

The cabinet is now ready for final sanding and finishing, but the information brochure with my aromatic cedar panels stated that the cedar should not be finished. Talk to your supplier of aromatic cedar so you'll get the best use from this fairly expensive wood.

Step 18. An inexpensive plastic-coated wire rack that allowed me to hang coats and store a few sweaters on the shelf was perfect for my requirements.

Step 19. The wardrobe is ready for final sanding and finishing.

Low-Cost Storage Shelving

I'm always looking for extra shelf space in the basement or workshop. Simply sticking together a few boards isn't always suitable because storage needs are always changing. I wanted a low-cost, adjustable shelf that could be moved if necessary.

A materials list did not seem appropriate for this project, as everyone's storage space is unique. Determine your requirements and adjust the dimensions accordingly.

PRO TIP

I plan to use particleboard for the shelves that are ¾"x11½"x31". These sizes maximize the cutting yield from a sheet of 4'x8' material. I suggest you do not exceed a shelf width of 32" unless you plan to add support braces. Heavy loads on a shelf that has a large span can bend or break the shelf board.

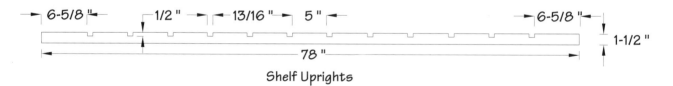

6-5/8 "		1/2 "	13/16 "	5 "		6-5/8 "	
			78 "				1-1/2 "

Shelf Uprights

Step 2. Cut the dadoes in the uprights ½"-deep by ¹³⁄₁₆"-wide. Start the first cut 6⅝" from the top, and space the dadoes 5" apart.

Step 3. Construct the shelf stretchers using 1½" square lumber.

Step 4. Connect the stretcher assemblies to four uprights with 2" wood screws in countersunk pilot holes.

Step 5. Cut and install the fixed shelves above the stretchers. Secure them with 2" wood screws.

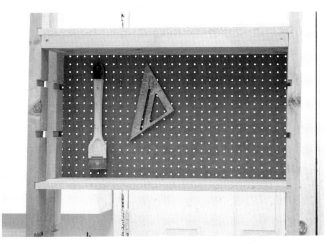

Step 6. Install the number of shelves required. If hanging storage is needed, add pegboard.

BUILDING THE SHELF

Step 1. Calculate the Upright Height

Measure the maximum height allowed in the area where you plan to keep the shelf unit. In my case, I had about 78" of free space in the basement storage room. For each shelf unit, I cut four uprights at 1½"x3½"x78". I made one unit with pressure-treated pine and the other with red cedar.

Step 2. Cut the Shelf Dadoes

Using my radial arm saw and a wobble dado blade, I cut grooves for the adjustable shelf system on the inside face of each upright.

Step 3. Build the Shelf Stretchers

Cut four boards at 1½"x1½"x8½". Cut another four at 1½"x1½"x30". Join two short and two long pieces with glue and 3" screws in pilot holes, forming a rectangle 11½"-deep by 30"-long.

Step 4. Connect the Uprights

Attach the stretchers to the four uprights using 2" wood screws. One stretcher assembly is secured directly below the top dadoes of each upright, the other is directly below the bottom dadoes.

Step 5. Install the Fixed Shelves

Cut two shelves at ¾"x11½"x31". Install one directly above the top stretcher and the other above the bottom stretcher in their respective dadoes. Secure the shelves to the stretchers with 2" wood screws.

Step 6. Cut the Shelves Needed

You can also add pegboard between two shelves to store tools and brushes. The shelf unit can be painted or left unfinished when using pressure-treated or cedar lumber.

Wine Storage Rack

Home wine making is a popular past-time. It is one of those hobbies that doesn't take too much time, allows you to enjoy the results and saves money. The downside is the ever-increasing number of bottles needing some form of storage. After being frustrated by dozens of wine bottles lying around my basement, I decided to design and build a wine rack.

I wanted a rack that tipped the bottles slightly downward to keep the corks moist. I also wanted to be able to read the labels easily. Here's the result—a 64-bottle rack that can be built in a weekend.

BUILDING THE WINE RACK

Step 1. Cut the Uprights

Cut the four uprights at ¾"x7"x58". Leave two at the full 7¼" as recommended in the project tip.

Step 2. Lay Out the Notches

Lay out the notch cuts, and make the cuts on a table saw.

Step 3. Join the Uprights

Attach one uncut upright to one notched upright with 1¼" screws and glue. Use two screws each at the top, middle and bottom, in countersunk, plugged holes. Assemble the uprights so the notched boards are mirror images facing each other.

Step 4. Assemble the Feet

Join the foot boards to form two assemblies, as shown on page 37. Use glue between each layer, and secure with two 2" screws.

Step 5. Notch the Foot Assembly

Cut a 1"-high by 7"-long notch on the bottom of each foot. This will help stabilize the rack on uneven floors.

PROJECT TIP

Leave the 1x8 boards at the 7¼" dressed width. Deepen the notches by ⅛" when cutting. Then trim the uprights to the finished 7" width, and you'll have perfectly square edges at the notches.

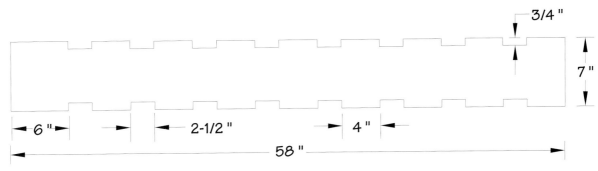

3/4 "

7 "

← 6 " →   ← → ← 2-1/2 " → ← 4 " →

← 58 " →

Rack Upright

Notch cuts are required on two of the four uprights.

Step 2. Cut the notches on a table saw equipped with a dado blade.

Step 3. Form the upright assemblies so the notched boards are mirror images of each other.

Materials List

This project is made from 1x8 knotty pine lumber. It is sometimes referred to as furniture- or #1 and #2-grade pine. However, any wood is suitable.

No.	Item	Dimensions T W L
4	Uprights	¾"x7"x58"
8	Foot boards	¾"x4½"x7"
2	Foot boards	¾"x7"x16"
4	Front racks	¾"x5⅛"x47"
4	Rear racks	¾"x7"x47"
4	Upright moldings	¼"x1"x52"
1	Top shelf	¾"x7¼"x52"
1	Top shelf back board	¾"x3½"x52"

Step 4. The feet are built-up ¾" boards with two 4½"-wide pieces per side, leaving a 7" space in the middle of the assembly.

 **PRO TIP**

When cutting the notches on a table saw, clamp a board behind the two uprights, so there will be minimal splintering on the project pieces as the saw blade exits the cut.

Step 6. Round over the feet with a ¼" router bit.

Step 7. Sand the uprights, and round over the outside face.

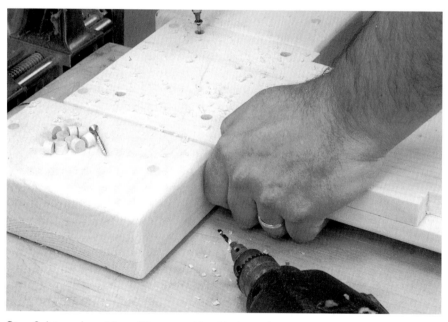

Step 8. Join each upright and foot assembly with glue and screws.

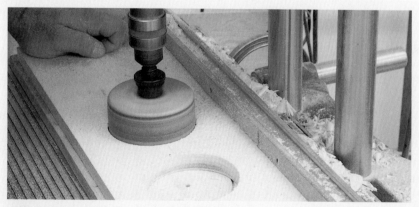

PRO TIP

To get clean, well-aligned holes, use a guide bar, and back the rack board with a scrap piece of lumber to minimize damage.

Step 6. Sand and Rout the Feet
Sand the foot assemblies smooth. Round over the edges of the assemblies with a ¼" roundover bit.

Step 7. Prepare the Uprights for Assembly
Sand the uprights, and round over the outside face with a ¼" roundover bit.

Step 8. Attach the Uprights to the Feet
Join each upright to a foot assembly with glue and four screws. Predrill and counterbore for the screw, and plug the holes. Align the bottom of the upright with the bottom of the cutout on the foot.

Step 9. Prepare the Front Racks
Cut four boards at ¾"x5⅛"x47". Drill eight 1½"-diameter holes, as shown on page 39.

Step 10. Prepare the Rear Rack
Cut four boards ¾"x7"x47". Drill eight 4"-diameter holes, as shown on the following page.

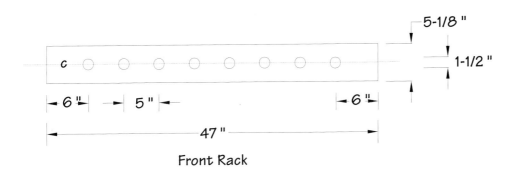

Step 9. Lay out the front rack boards, and drill the 1½"-diameter holes.

Front Rack

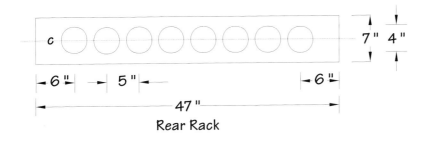

Step 10. Lay out the rear rack boards, and drill the 4"-diameter holes.

Rear Rack

Step 12. Cut the front and rear racks on a table saw as detailed.

Step 13. Secure the front and rear racks to the uprights with glue and finishing nails.

Step 11. Rip the Front Rack Boards

Cut the four front rack boards down the center. This will yield eight front racks at ¾"x2½"x47" with 1½"-radius arcs.

Step 12. Rip the Rear Rack Boards

Cut the four rear rack boards 2½" from each edge. You will then have eight rear racks at ¾"x2½"x47" with 4"-radius arcs.

Step 13. Attach the Racks

Glue and nail the rear and front racks to the uprights in the notches previously cut.

Step 14. Add the finishing touches by installing 1"-wide trim to the upright edges.

Step 16. Attach the top shelf assembly with glue and screws in plugged holes.

Step 15. Assemble the top shelf and back board.

Step 14. Add the Trim

Install a trim piece to each front and back face of the uprights. I used a 1"-wide piece of pine from the lumberyard.

Step 15. Assemble the Top Shelf

The top shelf assembly is made from two boards. The shelf board is ¾"x7¼"x52". The back board is ¾"x3½"x52". Sand both boards, and round over two ends and one edge of each piece with a ¼" roundover bit. Assemble with glue and 2" screws from the rear as shown.

Step 16. Install the Top Shelf

The shelf assembly can now be attached to the top of the uprights with glue and two 2" screws in predrilled, counterbored holes that are filled with wood plugs.

Step 17. Apply the Final Finish

I used a Minwax Provincial stain and two coats of polyurethane on the pine to complete my project.

Laundry Room Storage

In many homes, the laundry room seems to suffer from chronic lack of storage facilities. It's often an area in desperate need of good, organized cabinetry to keep the necessary laundry products.

In this chapter, we'll apply the traditional North American face-frame cabinet style in the laundry room. Traditional cabinetry expands on the standard European cabinet detailed in chapters one and two. We borrow on the sound box-building practices of the European system, and by adding a solid-wood face frame, we create a very strong, high-quality North American cabinet.

The cabinets will be built to suit the project laundry room, but they can be any size. The tables list all the necessary part sizes to build wall and base cabinets from 12" to 36" wide. We'll build an upper and base cabinet to demonstrate the procedures for each. Just pick the size that meets your requirements, and follow the assembly instructions. It's simple and beautiful cabinetry that's suitable for any room in your home.

The cabinet width is the outside dimension of the face frame—not the cabinet box. One word of caution with face-frame cabinetry: Be sure you cut the rails and cabinet boards accurately. The inside face-frame width is just a little smaller than the inside cabinet width to ensure the cabinet box (carcass) edges are fully covered. With the exception of that caution, building traditional cabinets for your home is a simple process.

The only parts not specified in any of the tables are the adjustable shelf sizes. They are normally cut $\frac{1}{16}$" shorter in overall width than the bottom board dimension. Cut as many as you'll need for each cabinet, and cover the edge with $\frac{5}{8}$" plastic shelf cap molding or iron-on edge tape. Both products are readily available in home stores.

I will build two 30"-wide upper cabinets for my laundry room project, and another that's 36" wide. The 36" base cabinet is fitted with a piece of post-formed countertop that is available as "shorts" or "end cuts" from a home store or countertop supply fabricator.

Cut and assemble the necessary parts of the box for the cabinets you wish to build. Follow the assembly instructions in the first two chapters. Predrill the screw holes. To achieve the best connection possible, use screws designed for joining melamine-coated particleboard, or use MDF or drywall screws with deep, sharp threads.

Traditional Face-Frame Cabinet Door Sizes

Cabinet Size & Type	Door Width	Door Height	# of Doors Required
12" Upper or Base	11½"	30½"	1
15" Upper or Base	14½"	30½"	1
18" Upper or Base	17½"	30½"	1
21" Upper or Base	10"	30½"	2
24" Upper or Base	11½"	30½"	2
27" Upper or Base	13"	30½"	2
30" Upper or Base	14½"	30½"	2
33" Upper or Base	16"	30½"	2
36" Upper or Base	17½"	30½"	2

Face Frame Cut List

Cabinet Width	Two Stiles (TWL)	Two Rails (TWL)
12"	¾"x1"x31¾"	¾"x1½"x10"
15"	¾"x1"x31¾"	¾"x1½"x13"
18"	¾"x1"x31¾"	¾"x1½"x16"
21"	¾"x1"x31¾"	¾"x1½"x19"
24"	¾"x1"x31¾"	¾"x1½"x22"
27"	¾"x1"x31¾"	¾"x1½"x25"
30"	¾"x1"x31¾"	¾"x1½"x28"
33"	¾"x1"x31¾"	¾"x1½"x31"
36"	¾"x1"x31¾"	¾"x1½"x34"

Upper Cabinet Materials List

Upper Cabinet Width	Two Sides	Top & Bottom	One Back
12"	⅝"x10⅝"x31"	⅝"x10⅝"x10¹⁄₁₆"	⅝"x11½"x31"
15"	⅝"x10⅝"x31"	⅝"x10⅝"x13¹⁄₁₆"	⅝"x14½"x31"
18"	⅝"x10⅝"x31"	⅝"x10⅝"x16¹⁄₁₆"	⅝"x17½"x31"
21"	⅝"x10⅝"x31"	⅝"x10⅝"x19¹⁄₁₆"	⅝"x20½"x31"
24"	⅝"x10⅝"x31"	⅝"x10⅝"x22¹⁄₁₆"	⅝"x23½"x31"
27"	⅝"x10⅝"x31"	⅝"x10⅝"x25¹⁄₁₆"	⅝"x26½"x31"
30"	⅝"x10⅝"x31"	⅝"x10⅝"x28¹⁄₁₆"	⅝"x29½"x31"
33"	⅝"x10⅝"x31"	⅝"x10⅝"x31¹⁄₁₆"	⅝"x32½"x31"
36"	⅝"x10⅝"x31"	⅝"x10⅝"x34¹⁄₁₆"	⅝"x35½"x31"

Building the Face Frame

Step 1. Attach the Face-Frame Members

Each cabinet face frame requires two ¾" stiles and two ¾" rails. The stiles are connected to the rails with glue and two 2" screws. Counterbore and predrill the screw holes; fill with wood plugs to match the frame. The drawings below and on page 44 illustrate how the frame is constructed and positioned on both upper and lower cabinets.

Step 2. Install the Face Frame on the Cabinet

Apply glue to the cabinet box edges, and place the frame in position, as shown in the drawings. Use 2" spiral finishing nails to face nail the frame in position. Make certain the frame's outside upper edge is flush with the outside top of the cabinet. Install the frame so it is equally overhanging the inside edges of the cabinet box.

Step 3. Fill the Nail Holes

The face-frame nail holes can be filled with a colored putty stick to match the finished color of the cabinets.

Assemble the melamine box pieces for the cabinet size required.

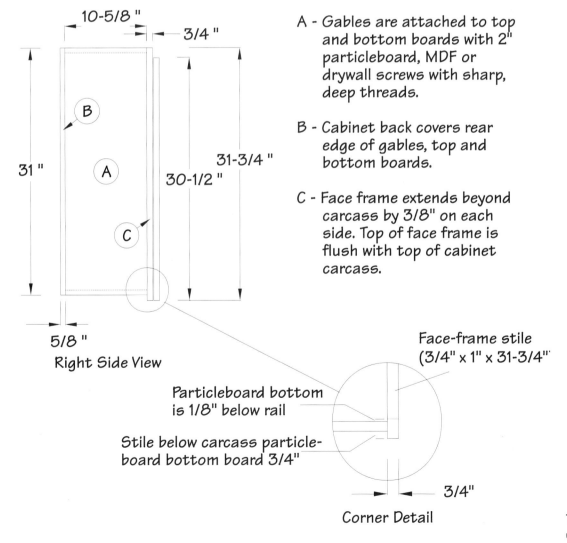

10-5/8 "

3/4 "

31 "

31-3/4 "

30-1/2 "

5/8 "

Right Side View

A - Gables are attached to top and bottom boards with 2" particleboard, MDF or drywall screws with sharp, deep threads.

B - Cabinet back covers rear edge of gables, top and bottom boards.

C - Face frame extends beyond carcass by 3/8" on each side. Top of face frame is flush with top of cabinet carcass.

Face-frame stile (3/4" x 1" x 31-3/4")

Particleboard bottom is 1/8" below rail

Stile below carcass particleboard bottom board 3/4"

3/4"

Corner Detail

The anatomy of an upper face-frame cabinet.

Step 1. The butt joints between the rails and stiles are secured with glue and 2" wood screws in counterbored holes.

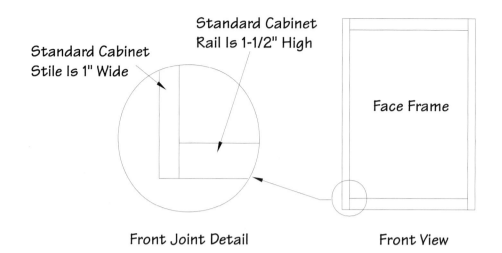

Standard Cabinet Stile Is 1" Wide

Standard Cabinet Rail Is 1-1/2" High

Face Frame

Front Joint Detail

Front View

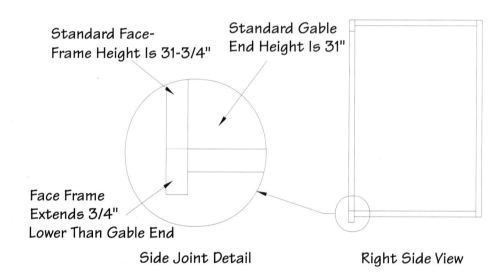

Standard Face-Frame Height Is 31-3/4"

Standard Gable End Height Is 31"

Face Frame Extends 3/4" Lower Than Gable End

Side Joint Detail

Right Side View

Step 2. Secure the face frame to the cabinet box with glue and 2" nails.

Step 3. Fill the nail holes with a putty stick.

Skill Builder   Building Cabinet Doors

Inexpensive cabinet doors can be made from any sheet material. For that matter, gluing up solid boards and cutting to the door size required is another popular method. In this chapter, I will be using oak veneer particleboard for the doors. In chapters one and two, I used melamine-coated particleboard. In chapter six, I'll be using oak veneer particleboard and adding a molding frame to change the look of the flat door.

Step 1. Apply Edge Tape
Cut the door material to the desired size, and apply to the door edges a preglued, heat-activated edge tape. Use a trimmer and fine sandpaper to trim the edge tape.

Step 2. Drill the Hinge Holes
Doors that are to be fitted with hidden or European hinges require a 35mm hole. I normally drill my holes ⅛" in from the door edge and 4" from each end. Each hinge manufacturer has slightly different hinge-mounting specifications, so check the recommendations with the hinge hardware.

Step 3. Install the Door Hinges
Most hidden hinges are installed with ⅝" screws through the holes in the hardware. To be certain the hinges are positioned correctly, use a square as a guide.

Step 1. Apply heat-activated edge tape to the door to cover the exposed surfaces.

Step 2. Drill the 35mm-diameter holes for the hidden hinges.

⚒ *Helping Hand* Building a Deadman

Step 1. Build a T and secure the joint with 3" screws.

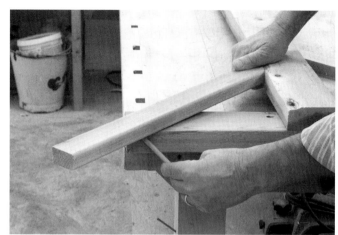

Step 2. Cut the angle supports flush at the top of the T.

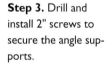
Step 3. Drill and install 2" screws to secure the angle supports.

Use the deadman to support upper cabinets during installation.

Positioning upper cabinets while securing them to the wall is a difficult task. Here's a little device many professionals use to make the task easier.

Step 1. Determine the Height

A deadman is usually 6" taller than the bottom of the upper cabinet when it's mounted in place. Most uppers are attached to the wall 54" above the floor, so I build my deadman 60" high. Cut the vertical 2x4 at 60" and the horizontal, or T member, to 24" long. Form a T with the pieces, and use two 3" screws to fasten them together.

Step 2. Determine the Support Angle

Cut two angle supports ¾"x1½"x20" with a 45° angle on one end of each board. Place the supports in the position shown, and mark the top angles flush with the top of the T.

Step 3. Attach the Angle Supports

Drill pilot holes to prevent the wood from cracking. Use 2" screws to secure the angle supports.

Step 1. Use four 3" screws to anchor the cabinet to the wall.

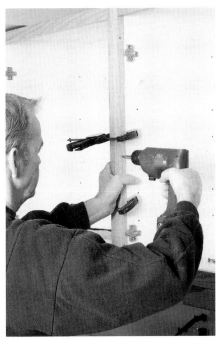

Step 2. Join the face frame with three 1½" screws.

Installing Upper Face-Frame Cabinets

Step 1. Secure the Cabinet

Place the cabinet in position, and verify it's level and plumb. Use a deadman or the help of an assistant. Attach the cabinet to the wall with four 3" screws. Make certain the screws penetrate a wall stud for maximum hold.

Step 2. Join the Cabinets

Face-frame cabinets, as well as being anchored to the wall, are attached to each other. Use 1½" screws at the top, bottom and in the middle of the stile. Drill a hole that's larger than the screw shaft in the stile closest to the screw head. This will cause the stiles to be drawn tightly together.

Step 3. Put the shelves in the cabinet, install the doors, and cover the exposed underside of the cabinets to complete the installation.

Step 3. Complete the Installation

Once the upper cabinets are in place, install the shelves and doors. For more detail on door installation procedures, see page 52. I often use a piece of ¼" veneer plywood to cover the underside of the cabinets for a professional, finished appearance.

Building and Installing Face-Frame Base Cabinets

Step 1. Construct the Base Carcass

Build the box (carcass) for the width of cabinet you require. For this application, I need a 36"-wide sink base cabinet. Join the sides to the bottom board, and attach the back as detailed in chapter one, page 12. Do not install an upper rail assembly as this part is only used for frameless base cabinets.

Step 2. Build the Face Frame

This base will feature a flip-out for extra storage. This means the face frame requires another rail positioned below the top rail, creating a 6" space. Assemble the face frame with glue and 2" wood screws.

Step 3. Install the Face Frame

Install the face frame as previously detailed. A base cabinet is different from an upper cabinet because it does not have a top board; therefore, the top edge of the frame must be aligned with the top edges of the cabinet sides. Both stiles will extend into the cabinet space by approximately ½". Position the frame so the overhang is equal from top to bottom.

Step 4. Mount the Doors

The doors on this cabinet are the regular 17½" width, but, because we are adding a flip-out tray, the height has been reduced to 23½". This measurement, plus the drawer face height of 6¾" and a ¼" space between the door and drawer, gives us the

Step 2. Build the face frame with an additional rail for a flip-out tray.

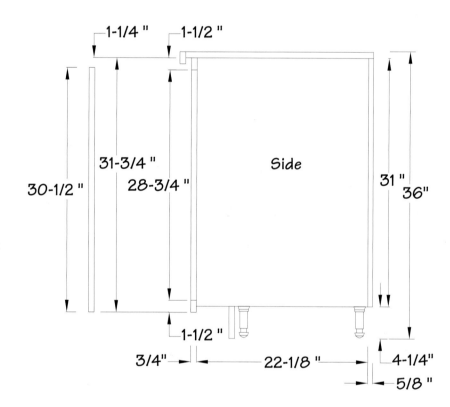

Drawing of a typical full-height door face-frame base cabinet.

standard 30½" height. For door installation information, see the Helping Hand on page 52.

Base Cabinet Cut List

Base Cabinet	Two Sides	One Bottom	One Back
12"	⅝"x22⅛"x31"	⅝"x22⅛"x10¹⁄₁₆"	⅝"x11½"x31"
15"	⅝"x22⅛"x31"	⅝"x22⅛"x13¹⁄₁₆"	⅝"x14½"x31"
18"	⅝"x22⅛"x31"	⅝"x22⅛"x16¹⁄₁₆"	⅝"x17½"x31"
21"	⅝"x22⅛"x31"	⅝"x22⅛"x19¹⁄₁₆"	⅝"x20½"x31"
24"	⅝"x22⅛"x31"	⅝"x22⅛"x22¹⁄₁₆"	⅝"x23½"x31"
27"	⅝"x22⅛"x31"	⅝"x22⅛"x25¹⁄₁₆"	⅝"x26½"x31"
30"	⅝"x22⅛"x31"	⅝"x22⅛"x28¹⁄₁₆"	⅝"x29½"x31"
33"	⅝"x22⅛"x31"	⅝"x22⅛"x31¹⁄₁₆"	⅝"x32½"x31"
36"	⅝"x22⅛"x31"	⅝"x22⅛"x34¹⁄₁₆"	⅝"x35½"x31"

Step 3. Install the face frame on the cabinet carcass.

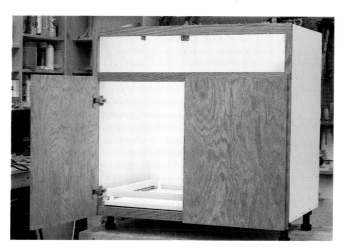

Step 4. Install the 23½" doors with hidden hinges.

🪚 PRO TIP

Drill a pilot hole when nailing through hardwood. The small bits are very hard and break quite often. You can save yourself a lot of wasted time looking for bits by using a nail as a drill bit. They do bend and break occasionally, but they're not very costly.

Step 5. The flip-out kit is simple to install and comes complete with installation instructions.

Step 6. Attach the open end panel with construction cement and brads.

Step 5. Add a Flip-Out Tray

The flip-out tray assembly is available from Rev-A-Shelf, Inc. and comes complete with hinges and mounting hardware. The drawer face is built in the same manner as a door and is as wide as the two doors.

Step 6. Install an End Panel

In cases where the ends of either base or upper cabinets are visible, install a ¼" veneer panel. Use construction adhesive and a few brad nails.

Step 7. Prepare the Base for Installation

This base unit will contain a sink, so holes must be cut in the back board for the supply and drain pipes. First measure the pipe locations, then cut the holes.

Step 8. Anchor the Cabinet

Level and plumb the cabinet before anchoring to the wall with 3" wood screws. If there are spaces between the cabinet and the wall, use cedar shims to fill the gaps. This will prevent any racking in the cabinet frame.

Step 9. Install the Countertop

Secure the countertop with ⅝" wood screws through right-angle metal brackets, as shown in chapter one.

Step 10. Locate the Sink

Follow the manufacturer's instructions and the template provided to cut the sink hole and complete the installation.

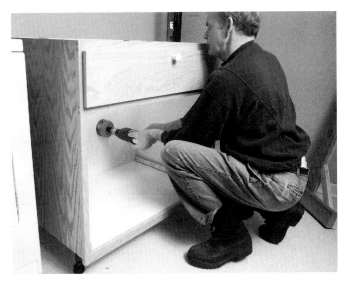

Step 7. Cut the holes for water supply and drain pipes.

Step 8. Anchor the cabinet to the wall with 3" screws.

Step 9. Install the countertop.

Step 10. Install the sink following the instructions provided by the manufacturer.

EDITOR'S NOTE

If you are interested in this hybrid style of kitchen and bathroom cabinetry, please refer to the author's book on the subject titled *Build Your Own Kitchen Cabinets*, published by Popular Woodworking Books. It is a very detailed building manual that includes all styles of kitchen cabinets including pantry, microwave, standard and special cabinets.

⚒ *Helping Hand* Installing Cabinet Doors With Hidden Hinges

Step 1. Mount the Hinges

Install the hidden hinges on the door as detailed in the Helping Hand on page 45.

Step 2. Align the Door

The hidden hinge is adjustable in three directions. The manufacturer sets all adjustments in the middle of their range; therefore, it's important that we attach the door to the cabinet as closely as possible to its final position. First, align the bottom of the door with the bottom of the cabinet. Then space the door about ³⁄₁₆" from the cabinet, with the hinge mounting plate in place on the hinge. I use a ³⁄₁₆"-thick strip of wood as my gauge. Insert two screws in each plate securing the door.

Step 3. Complete the Mounting Plate Installation

Now that the mounting plates are located, slide the door off the plates, and install the final screws.

Step 4. The Final Adjusting

Verify that the door is aligned and operates correctly. Slight adjustments may be necessary.

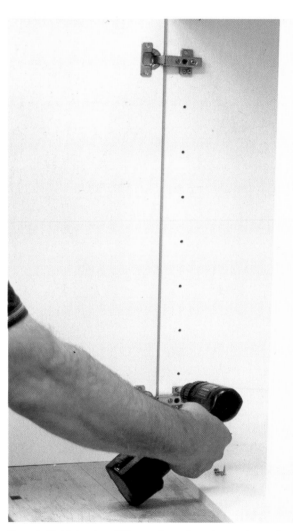

Step 2. Hold the door ³⁄₁₆" away from the cabinet edge, and insert ⅝" screws through the mounting plate into the cabinet side.

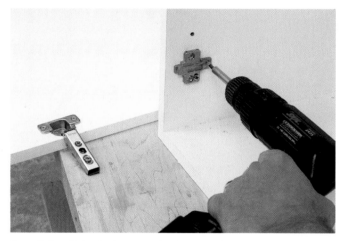

Step 3. Install the final screws after locating the mounting plates.

Step 4. Perform the final alignment and adjustment on the door.

Closet Storage Ideas

Building a Drawer/Shelf Tower

In this chapter, I'll provide you with a few ideas to help improve storage in your closets. Detailing exact measurements for all the projects would be of little value as everyone's closet is different, but I'll show you how to add valuable space and organization to any closet.

The center tower with drawers and shelves (shown above) is the core module with most closet systems. We want to make use of valuable space that often goes unused above and below the hanging rod. The tower is only 18" wide, but it creates a tremendous amount of storage space for sweaters and other garments. All other shelves and clothing racks are fixed to the side of this tower and a wall.

Step 1. Cut the Tower Side Panels

I have chosen to use white melamine-coated particleboard for this project. It's virtually maintenance free and is already finished. Cut two sides at ⅝"x23"x86", and apply white heat-activated melamine edge tape to the front edges.

Step 1. Cut the tower sides, and apply white edge tape to the front edges.

Step 2. Attach the horizontal supports with three 2" screws per side.

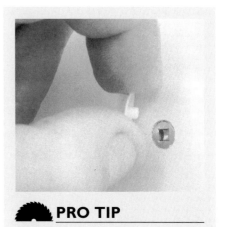

PRO TIP

Drive screws so the heads are flush to the surface. Use white screw cover caps, which are available at home centers, to hide the screws.

Step 3. Cut and install a toe-kick board.

Step 4A. Attach the upper back board.

Step 2. Install the Horizontal Supports

Cut three horizontal support boards to ⅝"x16¾"x23", and install. Apply edge tape, and use three 2" screws per side on each support. The screws should be designed to join particleboard, but can be MDF screws or drywall screws with deep, sharp threads. Remember to pre-drill the screw holes and drive them in until the head is flush with the outside surface. The lowest support is 2⅜" up from the bottom, the middle support is at 51", and the top support is flush with the top edge of the tower sides.

Step 3. Attach the Toe Kick

The toe-kick board is ⅝"x2⅜"x16¾". It is secured with one screw on each side and two through the top of the bottom support. Set the kick board 2" back from the front edge.

Step 4. Attach the Back Boards

Two back boards, one ⅝"x16¾"x33⅝" and the other ⅝"x3"x16¾", are attached to strengthen the cabinet. The tower will be anchored to the wall with 3" screws through these back boards. Use 2" screws and cover caps.

Step 4B. Attach the lower back board.

Step 5A. Assemble the four drawer boxes as detailed. Begin by joining the sides to the front and back boards.

Step 5B. Attach the drawer bottom with 2" screws about 6" apart. Predrill the holes, and cover all the exposed edges with tape.

BUILDING THE TOWER DRAWERS

Step 5. Cut the Drawer Parts

Construct four drawers from ⅝"-thick melamine particleboard pieces as listed in the cutting chart at right. Apply edge tape to the exposed edges. Attach the sides to the backs and fronts with 2" screws. Install the bottom board with 2" screws approximately 6" apart.

Step 6. Install Bottom-Mounted Drawer Glides

Install a set of 22" bottom-mounted drawer glides to each box. Start by installing the runners on the box, then attach the cabinet runners with 12" spacing. I made my drawer box 1" narrower than the inside tower width—according to the specifications with the Blum glides I'm using. Don't assume this dimension is standard with all manufacturers. Purchase the drawer glides

Step 6. Attach 22" bottom-mounted drawer glides to the cabinet and drawer bottom.

Materials List			
No.	**Item**		**Dimensions T W L**
8	Sides		⅝"x10"x22"
8	Backs		⅝"x10"x14½"
8	Fronts		⅝"x10"x14½"
4	Bottoms		⅝"x15¾"x22"
4	Drawer fronts		⅝"x12⅛"x18"

Step 7. Clamp the drawer fronts in place, and attach with 1" screws from inside the box. Install the fronts from bottom to top leaving a ¹⁄₁₆" space between them.

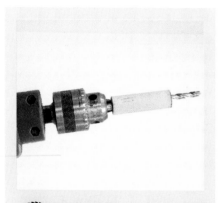

● PRO TIP

Make a drill stop from a wood dowel rod. Set it to the template's thickness plus ½" for perfectly drilled holes. More importantly, the stop prevents the drill from being pushed through the cabinet side board.

Step 8. Make a template, and drill the four columns of holes for the adjustable shelf pins.

Step 9. Cut the shelves, and cover the edge with ⅝" plastic cap molding.

before beginning construction to determine the required clearance.

Step 7. Install the Drawer Fronts

Secure the drawer fronts to the drawer box with two 1" screws through the drawer box and into the back of the drawer face. Mount the bottom drawer first, as shown at left, covering the bottom horizontal support. Continue attaching the drawer fronts from bottom to top, leaving a ¹⁄₁₆" space between them.

Step 8. Drill the Shelf Holes

The shelves will be sitting on adjustable shelf pins. Make a drill template from scrap wood, spacing the guide holes 3" apart. Use this template to drill holes in the upper section of the drawer tower.

Step 9. Make the Shelves

Cut three shelves to ⅝"x16⅝"x 22¼". Cover the front edge with ⅝" plastic cap molding. Secure the molding with construction adhesive.

INSTALLING THE CLOSET SYSTEM

There is another tower in the completed project, as shown on page 53. This narrow cabinet is a simple tall cabinet with a melamine door. The construction details are shown in chapters one and two. Use the base cabinet building steps and extend the height. However, this is a special application storage tower (for some tall, narrow items of mine) and isn't commonly used in most closet systems. Normally, a divider panel is installed to support an additional shelf system for shoes, as well as the hanging rods.

Step 10. Install the Tower

Start the closet installation with the drawer tower. Verify that it's level and plumb. Anchor the tower to the wall with 3" screws, through the back boards into the studs if possible.

Step 11. Add Divider Panels

You can install any number of divider panels in the closet system. Secure these panels in place with right-angle brackets attached to the floor and back wall.

Step 12. Install Shelves

I have added an additional column of shelves between an installed divider panel and the tower side. Use the shelf hole jig (page 26) and the procedures described in Step 8 for the adjustable shelf pins. These sets of extra shelving can be any width, depending on where the divider panel is installed.

Step 10. Secure the tower to the wall with 3" screws through the upper and lower back boards. Be sure the tower is level and plumb.

Step 11. Secure divider panels with brackets and screws.

Step 12. Add any number of shelf columns between the tower and divider panels.

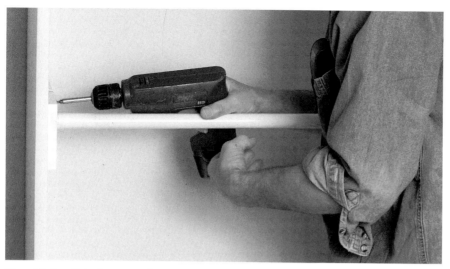

Step 13. Install the hanging rods using blocks of melamine particleboard. This method makes it possible to use longer screws to mount the rods.

Step 13. Attach the Hanging Rods

Commercially available white hanging rods can be found at most home stores. These can be adjusted to any width and are attached to the walls and divider panels with screws. I suggest you make square blocks of melamine particleboard to mount the rods into (see photo at left).

There are dozens of closet system accessories on the market. They range from simple wire shelving to the highest quality motorized rotary clothes-hanging systems.

Maximizing closet storage space is possible with a motorized system.

Wire hanging shelves and sliding drawer/shelf assemblies are available to help you get the most effective use of those small closet spaces.

Photo courtesy of White Home Products, Inc.

Photo courtesy of White Home Products, Inc.

Skill Builder Simple, Low-Cost Wall Shelving

Step 1. Cut the sheets of particleboard in 11½"-wide strips for the shelf and end boards. Join with glue and 2" screws.

There's always a need for low-cost shelving in the basement, work-shop, garage or cold storage room. Rather than spend a fortune on fancy veneer board or plywood, look at this particleboard applica-tion. I've built dozens of these shelf systems for family and friends.

Step 1. Cut the Sheet Goods

A 4'x8' sheet of ¾" particleboard cut into 11½"-wide strips will yield 32' of shelf material. Cut the strips to the desired length for the shelf boards and the desired width for the end boards. Join the shelves to the end boards with carpenter's glue and 2" screws made for particleboard, MDF or drywall joinery.

Step 2. Add Support Boards

I suggest you limit the shelf span to 36". Support boards are cut from the same material and butt joined with glue and screws. Use 2" screws in predrilled holes through the top and bottom shelves.

Step 3. Add Multilevel Shelving

If you plan to build multilevel shelv-ing, securing the support boards can be difficult. Use finishing nails with the heads cut off to help locate and prevent side movement of the support boards. Apply glue, locate the boards by gently tapping them onto the nails, then clamp in place until the glue sets.

Step 2. Limit the shelf span to 36" by adding support boards.

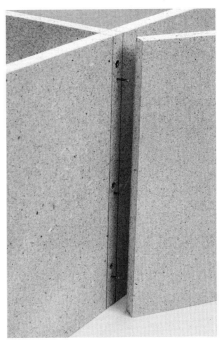

Step 3. Multilevel shelf support boards can be located with nails that have their heads cut off. Apply glue. Tap the board onto the nail and clamp.

Family Room Projects

Corner Entertainment Center

I've wanted a corner entertainment center ever since I built my family room addition, but I wasn't able to find one that suited my needs. First, the center had to contain the normal items such as a TV, stereo and VCR. But I also wanted storage for VCR tapes and compact discs, as well as a drawer for the spare cables, cleaning materials and manuals. After many weeks of searching, I decided to design and build one myself. If you're looking for a great corner unit with plenty of storage space, then here it is!

BUILDING THE CABINET

One word of caution before you start building this: make certain you have enough clearance through doorways in your home to move the cabinet. It's very large and can be awkward to move.

Step 1. Cut the Uprights

Cut four uprights from solid wood at ¾"x1⅜"x70" and angled at 22½° as shown in Figure 6-2 and the top left photo on page 61.

Step 2. Join the Uprights

Join the uprights with glue and biscuits, as shown in Figure 6-4.

Step 1. Cut four uprights with 22½° angles as shown.

Step 3. Attach the rails to the uprights. Two assemblies are required.

Step 3. Build the Side Frame

To form the sides, attach three oak rails ¾"x3½"x7" to a ¾"x1½"x70" upright, as detailed in Figure 6-6. Two assemblies are required. The simplest method of attaching the rails to the upright is with 2" screws through the upright into the rail ends. Counterbore the screw holes and fill with wood plugs.

Step 4. Attach the Angled Uprights

Join the angled uprights to the side frames using dowels or biscuits and glue. Clamp the frame assembly together until the glue sets.

PRO TIP

To help hold the uprights together during assembly, wrap tape tightly around them after inserting the biscuits and applying glue. The important joint is the outside angle, so get it as tight as possible.

Materials List

This project is made with solid oak and oak veneer particleboard shelving. However, any solid wood and sheet goods will work just as well.

No.	Item	Dimensions T W L
4	Uprights	¾"x1⅜"x70"
2	Uprights	¾"x1½"x70"
6	Rails	¾"x3½"x7"
1	Back panel	11/16"x32 5/16"x70"
1	Back panel	11/16"x33"x70"
3	Cross rails	¾"x3½"x30½"
2	Cross rails	¾"x1½"x30½"
2	Inside box backs	11/16"x8¾"x67½"
2	Inside box sides	11/16"x5"x67½"
8	Back board shelf cleats	¾"x¾"x27"
4	Rail shelf cleats	¾"x¾"x30½"
1	Oak veneer top before angle cutting	11/16"x36"x36"
3	Oak veneer shelves before angle cutting	11/16"x33"x33"
1	Bottom board before angle cutting	¾"x33"x33"
12	Compartment shelves	11/16"x4¼"x7⅞"
1	Drawer platform base	¾"x22"x18"
2	Drawer platform sides	¾"x2"x18"
2	Drawer box sides	11/16"x8 1/16"x18"
2	Drawer box fronts and backs	11/16"x8 1/16"x18⅛"
1	Drawer box bottom	11/16"x19½"x18"
1	Top edge oak trim	¾"x1½"x5'
1	Oak base frame	¾"x3½"x10'
2	Doors	11/16"x8"x41¼"
2	Doors	11/16"x8"x22¼"
1	Drawer face	11/16"x12"x31"
As needed	Door and drawer molding	32'

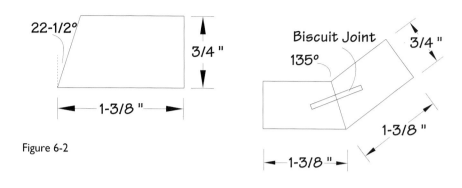

Figure 6-2

Figure 6-4

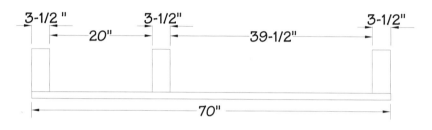

Figure 6-6

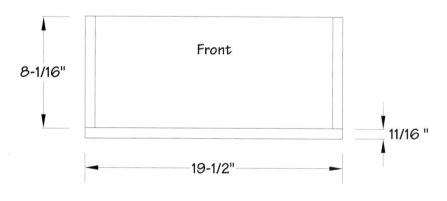

Front

Figure 6-11

Figure 6-12

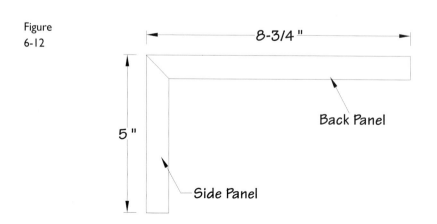

Back Panel

Side Panel

Step 5. Connect the Back Boards

Cut two back panels, as shown in the materials list. Attach as detailed in Figure 6-9, page 63. Use glue and 2" screws to join the panels.

Step 6. Attach the Side Frames

Join the side frames to the back panels, as shown in Figure 6-9. Use glue and four 2" screws in counterbored holes through the front of the face frame. Plug the holes with the appropriate wood plugs.

Step 7. Install the Cross Rails

Next, install the cross rails as shown in Figure 6-10. My rails are set so a 27" TV will fit in the center section. If you have another application, simply change the rail spacing dimensions. All my rails here are 30½" long. Be sure to have the side-frames-to-back-panel joint, as well as the back-panel-to-back-panel joint, blocked at 90°. Verify your measurement as it may vary slightly because of small dimensional differences when cutting the side frame members. It's not critically important for the rails to be exactly 30½". It is important that the 90° corners be accurate when taking

Step 5. Join the back panels with glue and screws.

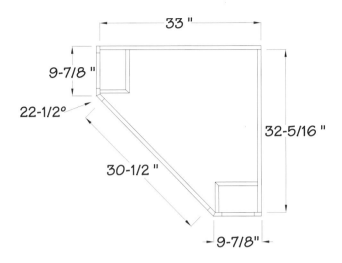

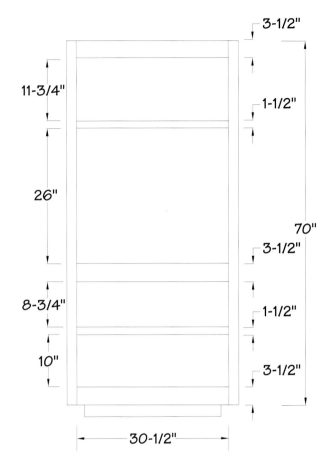

Figure 6-9

Step 6. Join the frames to the back panels with 2" screws through the front of each frame.

Figure 6-10

 **PRO TIP**

There will be corners that must remain at 90° during the assembly—for example, the right-angle joint for the back panels. Temporarily attach 90° corner blocks to maintain those angles until they are supported.

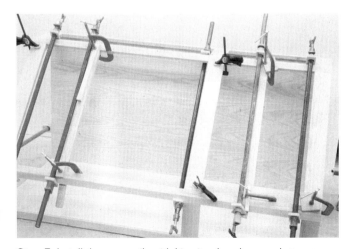

Step 7. Install the cross rails with biscuits, dowels or pocket screws and glue.

rail-length measurements. Install the rails with dowels or biscuit joints. You may need a helping hand at this point; getting all the rail-to-frame joints set, glued and installed can be challenging. Clamp the joints until the glue sets.

Step 8. Install the compartment box with glue and screws through the side frame and cabinet back boards.

Step 9. The wood shelf cleats are installed during shelf installation. They are shown in place for illustration purposes only.

Step 8. Build the Storage Compartment Box

The side and back panel assembly for the storage compartment is built with $^{11}\!/_{16}$" veneer particleboard shelving, as shown in Figure 6-12. Cut one edge of each panel to a 45° angle to form the corner. Join with glue and finishing nails. Put the box in place, and secure with glue and 2" screws through the face frame into the side panel, and through the cabinet back board into the edge of the box back panel. Install the box so its upper edge is flush with the top edge of the cabinet.

Step 9. Prepare the Shelf Supports

The three middle shelves and bottom board will be supported with ¾" square wood cleats. The lower left photo shows the cleats in position; but this is only to show the installation procedures. Install the cleats as you fit the shelves. You'll need a clear path to slide the shelves in place from the top of the cabinet.

Step 10. Cut the Bottom Shelf

All the shelves are cut by placing them on top of the cabinet and tracing the outline. There are three separate shelf patterns. The bottom shelf is cut to the inside perimeter of the cabinet, ignoring the compartment boxes. The middle shelves are also cut to the inside perimeter of the cabinet with a notch cut for the outside perimeter of the storage compartment boxes. The top shelf is the same pattern as the outside perimeter of the cabinet. Trace the outline for the bottom shelf. Install the shelf cleats above the shelf position, flush with the bottom edge of the compartment box. All the shelves, except the top, have three cleats: one cleat on each back panel, the third behind the front rail. The bottom board is ¾" particleboard shelving because it will be hidden by the drawer assembly.

Step 11. Install the Middle Shelves

Trace the pattern for the middle shelves and cut as accurately as possible. Install the three cleats for the first shelf, then slide in the shelf from the top. Install subsequent shelves the same way. If the shelf isn't cut clean, or there is damage from angle cutting the veneer board, use quarter-round molding around the shelf perimeter, as shown at center right. I've used a double-edged, rounded-over flat molding to hide any imperfections where the shelf meets the front rail.

Step 12. Finish the Frame

Round over all the inside and outside edges of the cabinet with a ⅜" roundover bit. Do not round over the cabinet top edge.

Step 13. Add Compartment Shelves

Cut as many compartment shelves as you require for your storage application. I will be storing video cassettes, but you may prefer to store compact discs. I've installed six shelves per side, spaced approximately 10" apart. Secure them in place with glue and 2" finishing nails through the cabinet back board, as well as the compartment side and back panel.

Step 10. Install the bottom shelf by securing it with glue and screws to shelf cleats. The cleats for this shelf are installed above the board, as the force from the base frame will be pushing upward on the boards.

Step 11. Install the three middle shelves. Quarter-round molding can be used around the perimeter of the shelf. The front shelf-to-rail joint can be covered with a flat molding.

Step 12. Dress all the hardwood edges, with the exception of the top edge, with a ⅜" roundover bit.

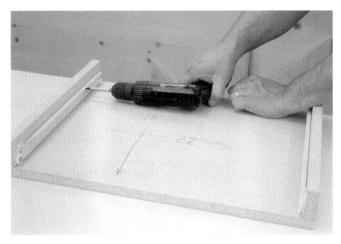

Step 14. Construct a drawer platform.

Step 15B. Test fit the drawer assembly.

Step 16. Cut and fit the top. Attach it with glue and finishing nails.

Step 15A. Build a drawer box, and install bottom-mounted drawer glides.

BUILDING THE DRAWER

Step 14. Build the Platform

The cabinet is angled, which means a platform must be constructed to support the drawer runners. The ¾" drawer platform dimensions are shown in the materials list. Join the sides to the platform base with glue and screws. Install the drawer runners, and screw the platform in place. The platform is installed directly behind the bottom rail, resting on the bottom shelf cleats. Use 1½" wood screws to secure the platform to the cleats. Center the drawer platform in the middle of the opening.

Step 17. Cut and attach the top trim boards.

Step 18. Install a 3½"-high base frame.

Step 15. Build the Drawer Box

Cut and assemble a simple drawer box that's 18" deep, as shown in Figure 6-11, page 62. Attach the bottom-mounted drawer glides. Verify that the drawer operates properly. You will need to apply a wood-veneer edge tape to the exposed edges of the particleboard shelving to complete the drawer.

Step 16. Install the Top

Cut a piece of ¹¹⁄₁₆" veneer particleboard shelving 36" square. Lay it on top of the cabinet, trace the outside perimeter on the board. Cut it to size. Attach it with glue and finishing nails to the top of the cabinet.

Step 17. Finish the Cabinet Top

Round over both edges on one face of a ¾"-thick by 1½"-wide board. Cut the necessary angles, and install on the front edge and both sides. Glue and face nail the trim, then fill the holes with a colored putty to match the final finish.

Step 18. Add a Base

I am installing a 3½"-high base frame, set back 3½" inside the cabinet perimeter. The frame is made

Step 19. Slab doors are made from veneer particleboard shelving. Molding is applied to add details to the door.

from 3½"-wide oak with a 2x4 support. Draw an outline 3½" back from the outside perimeter, and attach a 2x4 frame. Secure, on their edges, 3½"-wide oak boards to the frame.

Step 19. Make the Doors

I am using ¹¹⁄₁₆" veneer particleboard shelving with edge tape to make my

"slab" doors. To add detail, 1"-wide molding is attached to the door face 1" in from all edges.

Drill the necessary holes in order to run wire from each compartment, as well as a hole in the bottom for power supply. Sand and finish the cabinet. I applied three coats of oil-based polyurethane.

Modular Entertainment Units

This is a project where the dimensions are not as important as the design. One, two or three units, at different heights and widths, can be built to suit your needs. For example, two 6'-high modules with a 3'-high module in the center are a great combination for television and stereo equipment. It's also possible to add closed cabinets with doors or, as I have done in this project, a drawer unit with dividers for compact-disc storage. For this project, I've used birch hardwood and veneer board.

BUILDING THE POSTS

The most important design features of these modular units are the legs or posts.

Step 1. Make the Post Assembly

To make one 72"-high module, cut four pieces at ¾"x2"x72" and four pieces at ¾"x1¼"x72". Use either screws (covered with wood plugs) or biscuits to join the 1¼"-wide posts to the 2"-wide posts.

We want to join the post boards so we'll have four legs, forming a right angle, with two 2"-wide faces. To soften the look of the long posts, round over all outside edges.

Step 2. Make the Top and Bottom Fixed Shelves

The shelving is ¹¹⁄₁₆" veneer particleboard shelving with ¾"-square hardwood edging on all four faces. The wood strips are secured with glue and finishing nails. I've rounded over the top edges of the wood strips. My upper and lower fixed shelves are 20"-deep by 29"-wide.

Step 3. Install a Back Board

Before joining the fixed shelves to the posts, install a ¼"-thick back board. Cut the board 29"-wide by 70"-long, and attach it with glue and brad nails, so it's flush with the top of the posts. This position will leave a 2" space at the bottom of the posts. The back board serves two important purposes: it stops the module from twisting and racking, and it allows us to run wires from shelf to shelf through holes drilled in the back. These holes will be invisible behind the panel.

Step 1. Join the 1¼"-wide uprights to the 2"-wide uprights to make four "legs."

The uprights are joined at right angles forming a corner post with two 2"-wide outside faces.

Step 2. Make the top and bottom fixed shelves.

Step 3. Install a ¼"-thick back board joining two of the uprights.

Step 4. Assemble the Module

Install the top fixed shelf even with the tops of the posts. Use glue and 1½" screws through the posts into the shelves. Install the lower shelf 2" up from the bottom, and secure it in the same manner. Use a few nails to secure the edge of the back board to the upper and lower shelves. This will help stabilize the module.

Step 4. Assemble the modules.

Step 5. Build a drawer case from $^{11}/_{16}$" veneer particleboard shelving.

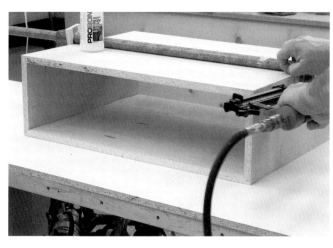

Step 6. Apply $^{1}/_{4}$"-thick hardwood finishing strips to the front edge of the drawer case.

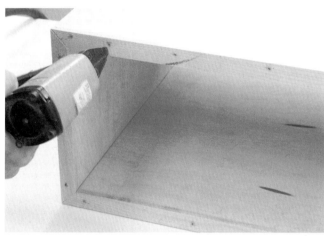

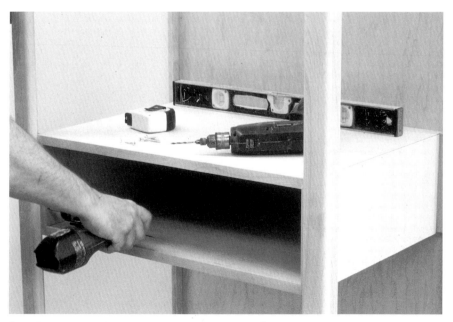

Step 7. Anchor the drawer case to the spacers with $1^{1}/_{4}$" screws through the inside of the case.

INSTALLING A DRAWER CASE

I had planned to store compact discs in a drawer assembly, so I attached a drawer at a comfortable height to view a television that will be placed on the case.

Step 5. Build the Drawer Case

The drawer case is built with two boards at $^{11}/_{16}$"x8"x19¾" for the sides. The top and bottom boards are $^{11}/_{16}$"x27"x19¾". Cut the boards so the corners are joined with a 45° miter cut. Secure with glue and finishing nails.

Step 6. Face the Drawer Case Edge

Cut and apply ¼"-thick by $^{11}/_{16}$"-wide strips of hardwood to the exposed edges of the drawer case. Attach with glue and brad nails. Fill the nail holes with wood putty.

Step 7. Install the Case

The drawer opening in the case must be inside the space between posts, so it's necessary to install ¾"x1"x8" wood spacers inside the posts. The drawer case will be aligned with these spacers and attached to them with screws. First, attach the spacers to the posts. Use glue with 1¼" screws, making sure the top edges of the spacers are at the same level on all posts.

BUILDING THE DRAWER

Any type of drawer box is suitable for this case. Refer to chapter eight, page 94, for details on building a Baltic Birch drawer unit. I cut slots in the front and back board of my drawer so I could stand compact-discs on end. Slot width depends on the storage requirements.

Step 8. Install a Drawer Face

Cut a drawer face ¾"x8"x26½". Round over the outside edges of the face with a ⅜" roundover bit in your router. Install the drawer front with two 1¼" screws from inside the drawer box.

Step 9. Drill the Shelf Pin Holes

Choose the type of adjustable shelf pin. Drill the holes about 2" apart, making sure they are properly aligned. Use a dowel stop on the drill bit to limit the hole depth.

Cut the required shelves using the same style of hardwood edge-banded shelves as used for the fixed shelves. But, the adjustable shelves are ⅛" less in width and depth to allow easy adjustment. I made four additional shelves measuring 19⅞"-deep by 28⅞"-wide.

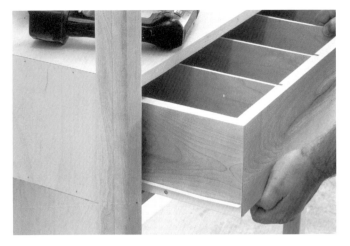

Cut slots in the front and back boards of the drawer box, and use pieces of ¼" wood as slip-in dividers.

Step 8. Cut a drawer face, round over the outside edges and secure with 1¼" screws.

Step 9. Drill adjustable shelf pin holes.

Firewood Storage Bench

This solid pine box is a beautiful addition to any "country style" family room. It is very popular and easy to build. It's made with 1x8 or 1x6 knotty pine boards glued up into panels. If you haven't done board "glue-ups," see chapter nine for details. Most firewood storage boxes are simply a place to hold logs, but, while serving a useful purpose, they do take up valuable seating space. I noticed my guests using the old firewood box as a seat during many family gatherings. That gave me an idea—why not make a box and bench combined? I think you'll find that it's a great addition to any room with a wood fireplace.

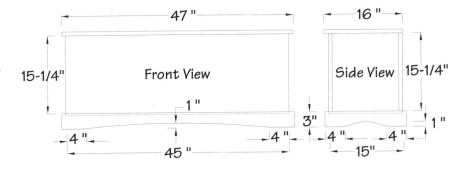

Drawings of box.

Materials List

All the wood panels are ¾"-thick pine.

No.	Item	Dimensions T W L
2	Sides	¾"x16"x45"
2	Ends	¾"x13½"x16"
1	Top	¾"x16"x47"
1	Bottom	¾"x13½"x43½"
1	Base skirt	1"x4"x14'

Step 1. Attach the front and back panels to the sides with glue and 2" wood screws.

Step 2. Install the bottom board with glue and screws through the box front, back and side panels.

BUILDING THE BOX

Step 1. Join the Panels

Sand all panels prior to assembly. Join the front and back panels to the side panels with glue and 2" wood screws. Always predrill the screw hole and counterbore so a wood plug can be installed. Use three screws per joint, spaced evenly along the front and back panels.

Step 2. Install the Bottom Board

Cut the bottom board to size, and secure with glue and screws. The panel is installed flush with the bottom edge of the box and screwed through the front, back and side panels.

Step 3. Make the Base Skirt

The base skirt is made up of four boards. The corner joints are at 45°, and the skirt parts are attached with glue and screws through the face in plugged holes. The skirt boards are installed so they overlap the box bottom by ¾". The notch in the skirt boards can be any design, but don't let the cut-out portion rise any more than 1½" above the bottom.

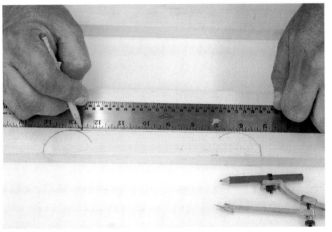

Step 3A. Draw the notch in each base board, and cut with a jig or band saw.

Step 3B. Secure the skirt boards to the box so it overlaps the bottom by ¾". Use glue and 2" screws in plugged holes.

Step 4. Round over the top edge of the skirt boards.

Step 5. Install the top using a piano hinge.

Step 6. Install a lid support.

Step 4. Complete the Skirt Board

Using a router, round over the top edge of the skirt board with a ¼" roundover bit.

Step 5. Install a Lid

Sand and round over the top and bottom front and side edges of a board that's ¾"x16"x47". This will allow the top to overhang the front and both sides of the firewood box by 1". Use small butt hinges or a strip of piano hinge to attach the top.

Step 6. Add Lid Hardware

I've installed a lid support mechanism to keep the box open. This feature is handy when taking fire logs out of the box. All that's left to do is apply a coat of your favorite finish. I used three coats of oil-based polyurethane, which turns the pine a golden honey color that so many people admire. Sew a cushion from material to match your decor. The cushion can be held in place with "peel-and-stick" strips so it won't fall off when the box lid is opened.

𝄞 *Helping Hand*   Helpful Tips

Pipe Clamp Pads

Pipe clamps are one of the most useful woodworking tools anyone can own. Still, I was always looking for wooden blocks to prevent the clamp jaws from damaging my project. Here is a simple idea that really improved my clamps. Drill a hole through a block of ¾" wood that's large enough to cover the clamp face. Slip blocks between the jaws and you'll always have them ready for use.

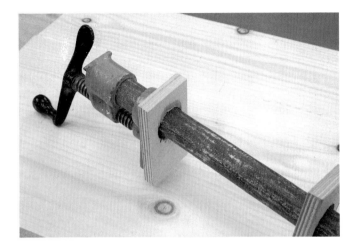

Homemade "soft jaws" for your pipe clamps.

Gluing 45° Joints

Do you need help gluing up 45° miter joints? Here's a little trick that can save a lot of frustration. Lay the boards flat with the miter down. Apply masking tape tightly over the two boards spanning the joints. Turn the boards over, and brush on the glue. Close the joint. The tape will hold both boards tightly in place until the glue sets.

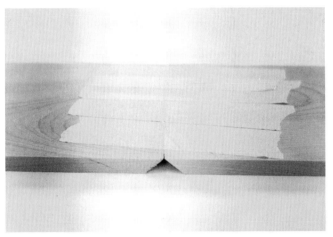

Masking tape acts like a clamp and holds miter joints together while the glue dries.

Cutting Veneer Sheet Goods

Cutting expensive veneer boards with anything other than the proper blade in the table saw can damage the veneer. To prevent this from happening, score the cut line with a utility knife. Press hard enough so the veneer layer is cut completely. Then, when using a jigsaw or circular saw, the tear-out will be minimal.

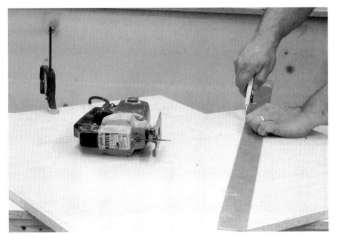

Score the cut line before cutting expensive wood veneer-covered boards with a jig or skill saw.

Improving Bathroom Storage

Vanity Base With Towers

Most bathrooms are small and present quite a few challenges when trying to improve storage. It's a real problem for families with children because of all the necessary items used in the bathroom each day. Linen, toiletries, soaps and paper products all take up room. The average bathroom vanity is two or three feet wide. Sometimes it has small drawers, and very rarely does it have adequate space under the sink—that area is usually taken up by the leaky plumbing pipes. I can't do anything about leaky plumbing pipes, but I will show you one or two ideas on regaining some valuable storage space in your bathroom. Tall bathroom cabinets can be very useful, and a single-sink vanity to contain the plumbing separates the wet, or potentially wet, and dry areas.

The space over a toilet is prime storage space and a great place to add a wall cabinet. There's often a blank wall where a towel bar is located, which is easily replaced with a towel storage rack. I'll start this chapter with a unique project that replaces a five-foot vanity with a single sink base and twin storage towers.

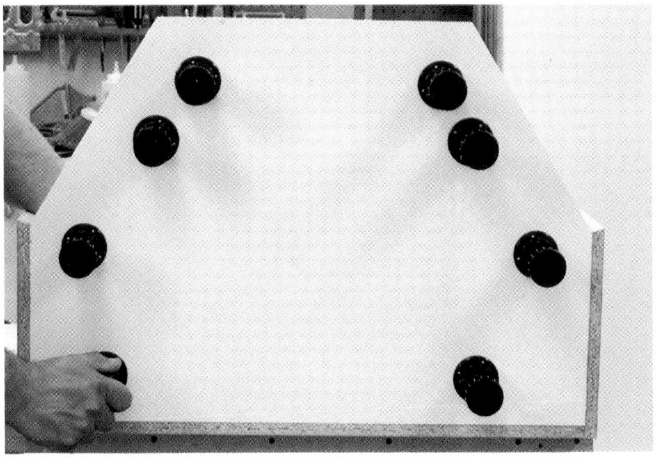

Step 4. Install a base platform using cabinet leg levelers or a wood 2x4 frame.

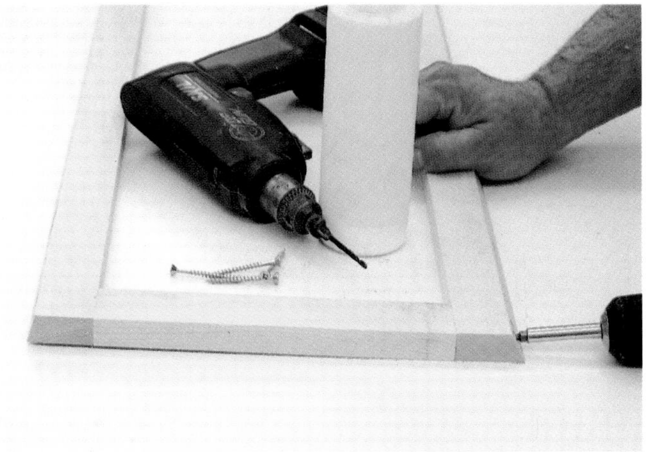

Step 5. Join each section of the face frame with glue and 2" wood screws.

BUILDING THE VANITY BASE

Step 1. Cut the Base Board Angles

Cut a base board for the vanity from ⅝" white melamine particleboard shelving with the angles and dimensions as shown in Figure 7-3 on page 78.

Step 2. Cut the Back Board

The cabinet back board is melamine particleboard shelving ⅝"x28"x28¾". The back board doesn't require any angle cuts.

Step 3. Prepare the Sides

Two cabinet sides are needed. They must be ripped with an angle on one long side, as shown in Figure 7-4. Once all the parts are cut, assemble the cabinet, as shown in Figure 7-3, and at top left (step 4) on this page. Use 2" screws, designed for particleboard joinery, in predrilled holes. Space the screws about 6" apart.

Step 4. Build a Base Platform

You can either install base cabinet leg levelers or build a 2x4 platform faced with maple hardwood. Either method is acceptable. Set back the

Materials List

This project is built with maple hardwood and 11/16" maple veneer particleboard shelving. The interior of the vanity cabinet is constructed with ⅝"-thick white melamine particleboard shelving. It's finished with three coats of water-based clear polyurethane. The doors are made with ¾"x1½" maple veneer particleboard. The center panels are ½"-thick. All stiles and rails have the ends cut at 45°, and the measurements given are at the longest dimension.

No.	Item	Dimensions T W L
1	Vanity base board	⅝"x20"x28¾" (before angle cuts)
1	Vanity base back board	⅝"x28"x28¾"
2	Vanity base sides	⅝"x12"x28" (before angle cuts)
2	Vanity base panels	½"x11½"x27¼"
6	Vanity face-frame stiles	¾"x1½"x28¾"
4	Vanity face-frame rails	¾"x1½"x9⅛"
2	Vanity face-frame rails	¾"x1½"x13"
4	Tower sides	11/16"x11¾"x80"
2	Tower backs	11/16"x11⅞"x80"
4	Tower tops/bottoms	11/16"x10½"x11¾"
12	Tower shelves	11/16"x10⅜"x11¾"
4	Door stiles	¾"x1½"x80"
4	Door rails	¾"x1½"x11½"
2	Door stiles	¾"x1½"x28"
2	Door rails	¾"x1½"x14"
2	Door center panels	½"x9⅛"x77⅝"
1	Door center panel	½"x11 1/16"x25 9/16"
1	Backsplash	1"x3" as needed

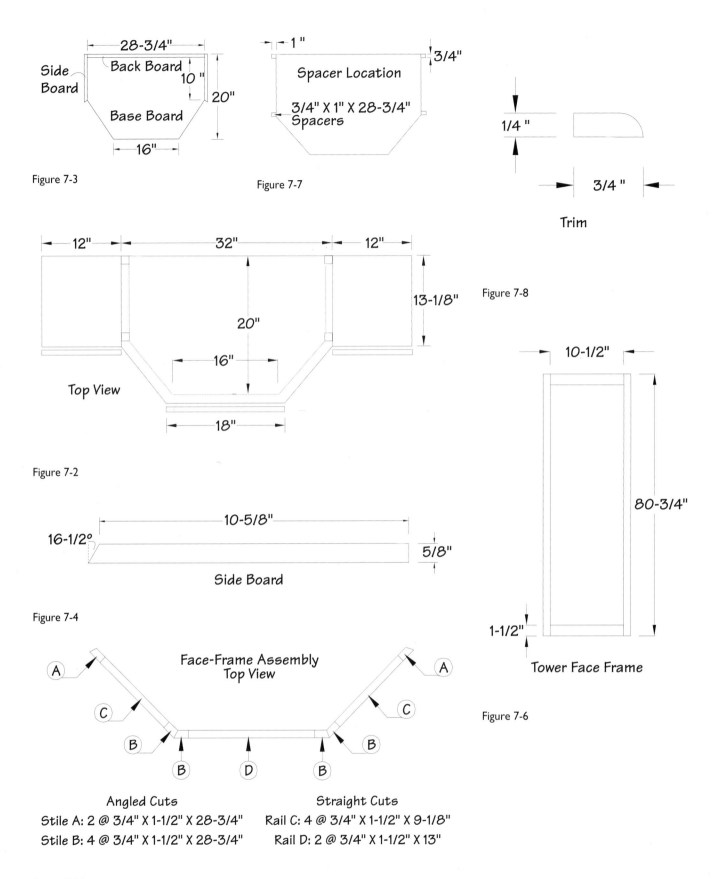

Figure 7-3

Side Board

Back Board

28-3/4"

10"

20"

Base Board

16"

Figure 7-7

1"

3/4"

Spacer Location

3/4" X 1" X 28-3/4" Spacers

Figure 7-8

Trim

1/4"

3/4"

Figure 7-2

Top View

12"

32"

12"

13-1/8"

20"

16"

18"

Figure 7-4

Side Board

10-5/8"

16-1/2°

5/8"

Figure 7-6

Tower Face Frame

10-1/2"

80-3/4"

1-1/2"

Figure 7-5A

Face-Frame Assembly
Top View

A

C

B

B

D

B

A

C

B

Angled Cuts
Stile A: 2 @ 3/4" X 1-1/2" X 28-3/4"
Stile B: 4 @ 3/4" X 1-1/2" X 28-3/4"

Straight Cuts
Rail C: 4 @ 3/4" X 1-1/2" X 9-1/8"
Rail D: 2 @ 3/4" X 1-1/2" X 13"

base platform from the front and sides of the cabinet by 3" to provide toe-kick space.

Step 5. Build the Face Frame

The base cabinet face frame is three wood frames joined together. You will need to rip the stiles (vertical frame members) at the angles shown in Figure 7-5 on page 78. Use 2" screws and glue to hold each section together before attaching the three sections. These holes aren't plugged, as they will be hidden.

Step 6. Join the Frames

The three face-frame sections can be secured with #0 biscuits. Once they are installed and glue is applied, wrap masking tape around the stiles until the glue dries.

Step 7. Install the Face Frame

Attach the face frame to the cabinet using glue and 2½" spiral finishing nails. The nails are driven through the face of the frame into the cabinet base board and sides. The top edge of the face frame must be flush with the top edge of the cabinet sides. Notice that the side stiles at the cabinet side boards extend slightly past the edge. That is due to the joint between two different thicknesses of material. However, that situation is good in this case because we will be installing spacers later in the project that will rest against this lip.

Step 6. Connect the face-frame sections with #0 biscuits and glue. Tape tightly until the glue dries.

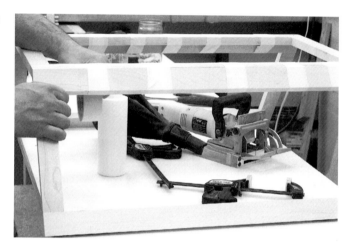

Figure 7-5B. Labels A and B refer to the vanity face-frame stiles in Figure 7-5A.

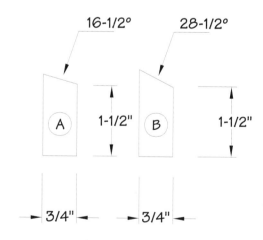

Step 8. Round over the inside edges of the side face frames.

PRO TIP

The face-frame stiles have to be ripped at an angle, and the indicator on most table saws isn't always accurate enough. To set the table saw blade, cut a block to the desired angle with a power miter saw, and use it as a gauge to set the blade.

Step 8. Round Over Face Frame

Round over the inside edge of the two side face-frame openings. Use a ⅜" roundover bit. Complete sanding the face frame.

Step 9. Install the Face-Frame Panels

The panel must completely cover the opening, so check the dimensions before cutting and adjust accordingly. Cut two panels from veneer particleboard ½"x11½"x27¼". Install them in the side face-frame openings from the interior of the cabinet. Use glue and 1" brad nails.

Step 10. Install Cabinet Spacers

Next, ¾"x1"x28¾" spacers must be attached to the cabinet sides. Four spacers are required as shown in Figure 7-7 on page 78. They are secured to the cabinet sides with 1½" screws. One is installed at each back corner and one directly behind and tight to the back edge of the face frame at the frame-to-cabinet-side intersection. These spacers are required so the countertop edge can meet the tower cabinet sides behind the tower face frames.

Step 11. Install Countertop Clips

Install seven right-angle countertop clips in the base cabinet. They will be needed when attaching the top.

Step 12. Cut the Countertop

Temporarily attach an ¹¹⁄₁₆"-thick piece of particleboard shelving to the cabinet top. Trace the perimeter of the cabinet on the underside of the board. Draw the line straight from spacer to spacer and tight to the front of the face frame. Remove the board and cut the countertop.

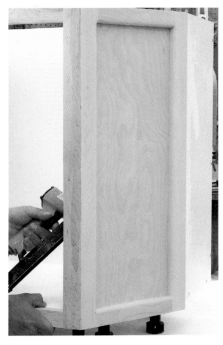
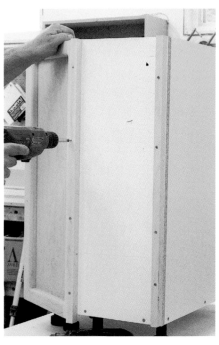

Step 9. Install the side panels from the cabinet's interior. Use glue and 1" brad nails.

Step 10. Install spacers as shown with 1½" screws into the cabinet side boards.

Step 11. Install seven countertop clips around the top perimeter of the base.

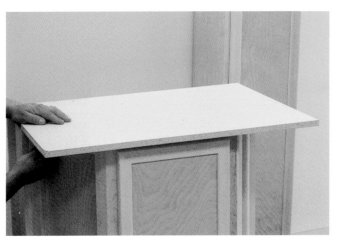

Step 12. Trace and cut the countertop substrate board to size.

Step 13. Install a hardwood edge on the sides and front of the countertop board. Sand flush the edge of the hardwood that extends past the top's side.

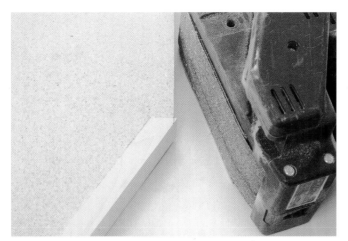

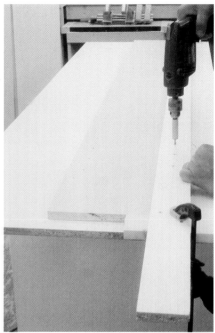

Step 17. Drill two columns of holes in each tower side to accept the adjustable shelf pins.

Step 14. Sand the hardwood edge and top smooth. Soften the front corners with a sander.

BUILDING THE TOWERS

Step 16. Cut the Parts

Cut all the necessary tower cabinet parts from $^{11}/_{16}$" maple veneer particleboard shelving (see materials list).

Step 17. Drill Adjustable Shelf Holes

Before assembling the towers, holes must be drilled on the inside face of each cabinet side for the adjustable shelf pins. Accurate hole placement is important. To ensure accuracy, a shelf hole jig can be made from a scrap piece of lumber. Set the holes as far apart as you prefer. For this application, I've spaced my holes at 3" on center. Clamp the jig to a tower side, and drill two columns of holes in each side. Use a wood dowel on the drill bit as a stop gauge. Place each column of holes 1" in from each edge.

Step 13. Add a Wood Edge

Attach a ¾"-thick by 1¼"-wide piece of maple hardwood to the two angled sides and front edge. Use glue and screws through the front edge of the hardwood. The holes will later be filled with wood plugs. The hardwood edging at the back of the angled sides will extend past the side of the board. Draw a line along the side, through the hardwood edge, and sand flush with a belt sander.

Step 14. Complete the Top Edge

Sand the face of the hardwood edge, making sure the top is smooth. Use a sander to slightly round and soften the front corner joints of the edge.

Step 15. Apply the Laminate

Refer to chapter two, page 23, and install the laminate to match your decor.

Step 18. Join two tower sides to a top and bottom board. Use glue and 2" screws making sure that the shelf pin holes are aligned from side to side panel.

Step 19. Install the tower backs with glue and 2" screws.

Step 18. Join the Tower Sides

Assemble the tower carcasses by attaching two sides to a top and bottom board. Use glue and 2" particleboard screws in predrilled holes. These screws will be covered with trim molding when the cabinets are installed. The top and bottom boards are flush with the ends of the sides. Make certain the shelf pin holes are correctly oriented with each other.

Step 19. Install the Tower Back

Attach the tower backs to each unit. Use glue and 2" screws placed about 8" apart.

Step 20. Construct a Tower Base

Install cabinet-leg levelers (that will have clip-on toe-kick boards installed) or a 2x4 base frame covered with maple. Set the base frame 3" back from the front edge of the cabinet to provide a toe-kick space.

Step 20. Install base cabinet levelers or a wood frame that's 3½" high. Set the frame back 3" at the front of each cabinet to provide toe-kick space.

BUILDING A TOWER FACE FRAME

Step 21. Assemble the Face Frame

Build a face frame for each tower according to the dimensions shown in Figure 7-6 on page 78. Attach the stiles to the rails with simple butt joints using glue and 2" screws in counterbored holes. Plug any visible holes with wood plugs.

Step 22. Install the Face Frames

Attach the face frames to the tower carcasses with glue and 2½" spiral finishing nails through the face of the frame. The top edge of the face frame is set flush with the top edge of the cabinet. The inside face of each stile should be flush with the inside surface of the side board.

Step 23. Cut Tower Shelves

Use ¹¹⁄₁₆" maple veneer particleboard shelving and cut as many shelves as you require. The front exposed edge of the shelves are covered with preglued heat-applied wood edge tape. This edging is installed with an iron and pressure roller. It's available in a ¾" width, and the excess is trimmed with a sharp knife. For my towers, I cut twelve shelves ¹¹⁄₁₆"x10⅜"x11¾". It's worth repeating: check the measurements on your cabinets before cutting the shelves.

Step 21. Build the face frame using glue and 2" wood screws in counterbored holes. Plug any visible holes with wood plugs.

Step 22. Attach the face frame to the tower carcass with glue and 2½" spiral finishing nails. The top edge of the face frame is flush with the top of the carcass. The inside edges of the faceframe stiles are flush with the tower sides' inside surface.

BUILDING THE DOORS

The doors used on these cabinets are a modified version of the slab door. Slab doors are simply $1\frac{1}{16}$"-thick veneer particleboard shelving with applied edge tape. These doors must be strong because they are tall. A hardwood frame, with $\frac{1}{2}$"-thick veneer particleboard as the center panel, was designed for this application. They also differ from standard kitchen or vanity cabinet doors because the corners are mitered at 45°.

Step 24. Cut the Stiles and Rails

Rough cut all the stiles and rails for the three doors. By "rough cut" I mean leaving them a little longer than necessary, so you can do a clean 45° miter cut after the rabbet has been completed.

Step 25. Rabbet the Door Frame

First, round over both edges on one face of each board with a $\frac{3}{8}$" router bit. Next, plow a rabbet on the opposite side of all stiles and rails. Use a router or dado blade in a table saw. Cut the rabbet $\frac{1}{2}$"-wide by $\frac{1}{2}$"-deep.

Step 26. Join the Door Frame

Cut a 45° miter on both ends of each stile and rail. Cut to the finished dimension shown in the materials list. Assemble the frames with glue and brad nails. You will have two doors at $11\frac{1}{2}$"-wide by 80"-high and one at 14"-wide by 28"-high.

Step 27. Install the Door Panels

Prepare three $\frac{1}{2}$"-thick maple veneer particleboard panels for the door frames. Two are $9\frac{1}{8}$"-wide by

Step 25. Round over both edges on one face of each stile and rail. Then cut a $\frac{1}{2}$"x$\frac{1}{2}$" rabbet on each face as shown.

Step 26. Assemble the door frame with glue and brad nails.

$77\frac{5}{8}$" high, and one is $11\frac{1}{16}$"-wide by $25\frac{9}{16}$"-high. Verify your measurements before you cut the panels. They should fit tight in the door frame. Secure with a little glue and $\frac{5}{8}$" brad nails.

Step 27. Cut and install three panels in the door frames.

Cut wood strips to install on the cabinet sides.

INSTALLING THE DOORS

Follow the procedures in chapter two, page 45, on how to install hidden hinges and install cabinet doors.

CABINET INSTALLATION NOTES

Prior to installation, prepare a countertop backsplash. It's simply 1"x3" hardwood that has been rounded over on the top outside edge. Install the backsplash with screws in holes covered with wood buttons. In case removal is necessary, do not glue them in place. The corners where the two sides meet the back board are joined at 45°. A small trim molding can be inexpensively made from a piece of ¾"-thick stock. Round over one edge, as shown in Figure 7-8 on page 78, and cut the ¼"-thick strips on a table saw.

These trim pieces are attached around the visible sides of all the cabinets. They cover imperfections on the wall and hide the screws used to assemble the cabinets. The rounded-over edge is installed facing inwards.

Cabinets must be installed level and plumb. The fit and finished appearance depends a great deal on how carefully the cabinets are installed. When you are confident the positioning is accurate, secure the cabinets to the wall studs with 3" wood screws. Install 3½"-high hardwood kick boards on the cabinet legs. Or, if you've used a 2x4 platform for the base, attach the hardwood face boards.

Figure 7-31

Figure 7-32

Bathroom Cabinet Ideas

WALL-TO-WALL STORAGE

This cabinet is made of solid 7"-wide oak and was designed to completely fill a space above the toilet. It's a simple frame with a fixed middle shelf and adjustable interior shelves. The back board is ¼" oak veneer plywood. I purchased fancy raised-panel doors and attached them with hidden hinges. It's a great cabinet for linen storage (Figure 7-31).

PARTICLEBOARD CABINETS

Here's another simple wall cabinet built with ¹¹⁄₁₆" veneer particleboard shelving. It has a lower fixed shelf and adjustable interior shelves. I installed upper and lower nail

boards in place of a back board. The cabinet is hung from these boards. The door is a simple slab door made from the same ¹¹⁄₁₆"-thick veneer particleboard shelving with taped edges. The door was tole painted with a design, and European hidden hinges were installed (Figure 7-32).

SPACE-SAVING WALL CABINETS

When there's very little space, an over-the-toilet cabinet is the perfect solution. They can be made any size, and even the smallest cabinet can hold a great number of toilet products. This cabinet is also a good solution when children are in the home because it's up and out of the way. A lock can be installed to safely store medicines and other potentially dangerous products (Figure 7-33).

Figure 7-33

Figure 7-35

Figure 7-36

Figure 7-34

SIMPLE BASE CABINETS

Simple base cabinets can be built using the techniques explained in chapters one and two. This cabinet is made from $^{11}/_{16}$"-thick oak veneer particleboard. It has plastic leg levelers installed to isolate the wood from the sometimes-damp basement floor. The countertop was an

"end cut" I bought at a savings from a local supplier. As with all vanity cabinets, there isn't much room for anything but the plumbing, so in that sense these are not good storage units. However, there's always room to store cleaning products. It has a slab door that has been tole painted and mounted on hidden hinges. All in all, I spent about $60 Canadian for the materials (Figure 7-34).

TOWEL RACK STORAGE

Towels are normally hung on a simple bar rack that takes up a lot of wall space and provides very little storage. Here's an idea to increase that storage with just a few pieces of wood. This rack is made from 1x6 maple hardwood. 1" dowel rods are installed to hold three towels, and adjustable shelf pin holes were drilled to hold shelves. The rack

doesn't take up any more room than the towel bars but provides much more storage area (Figure 7-35).

TALL CABINETS

If you have 18" to 24" of free wall space in your bathroom, consider building a tall cabinet. It's nothing more than an upper and a base cabinet. The cabinet sides are full height with fixed shelves positioned to match the door heights. It's only 12" deep but capable of storing quite a lot of bathroom products. These doors are commercially made, but installing slab doors can reduce the cabinet construction cost. Look around your bathroom; if you've got a little free wall space this may be your best storage solution (Figure 7-36).

Master Bedroom Storage Projects

Television Armoire

This project is the start of a series of similarly styled bedroom storage furniture. The television armoire is now a popular item in most large bedrooms. Nothing is nicer than enjoying your morning coffee in bed while watching TV. But that ugly television, with all the necessary wires and equipment, is a real eyesore. This cabinet will provide hidden storage for the TV and give you some large storage drawers as a bonus.

Don't let the complex-looking doors stop you from building this

or any other project in the chapter. It's just a matter of putting sticks together—one piece at a time.

BUILDING THE CABINET

Step 1. Prepare the Side Panels

Cut a rabbet in the side panels that is ⅜"-deep by ¾"-wide on the inside back of each side panel and the bottom of each panel. Next, cut a ⅜"-deep by ¾"-wide dado 24" up from the bottom edge to accept the middle fixed shelf.

Step 2. Attach the Back Board

Clamp the back board, between the side boards, in the rear rabbets. Secure with glue and 2" spiral finishing nails approximately 8" apart.

Step 3. Install the Fixed Shelves

Glue and nail the bottom shelf in place by nailing from the bottom face into the side boards. Then drive 2" screws through the back board into the bottom shelf. Clamp the middle shelf in the dado. Install the shelf cleats under the shelf. Secure them with glue and 1¼" screws into the side and middle shelf boards. Install 2" screws through the back board into the shelf.

Materials List

The sheet goods are ¾"-thick oak veneer particleboard shelving, and the hardwood is ¾" oak unless otherwise noted.

No.	Item	Dimensions T W L	Materials
2	Sides	¾"x23"x53½"	Particleboard shelving
1	Back	¾"x33¼"x53½"	Particleboard shelving
2	Shelves	¾"x22¼"x33¼"	Particleboard shelving
2	Side cleats	¾"-thick by 22¼"-long	Oak
1	Back cleat	¾"-thick by 31"-long	Oak
2	Stiles	¾"x1½"x53½"	Oak
3	Rails	¾"x1½"x31"	Oak
1	Rail	¾"x¾"x31"	Oak
1	Base board	¾"x3½"x31"	Oak
2	Base boards	¾"x3½"x20"	Oak
1	Base board	¾"x3½"x29½"	Oak
1	Top	1"x25"x36"	Oak
2	Doors	¾"x15⅜"x27"	Particleboard shelving
1	Top cleat	¾"x1½"x32½"	Oak
22"	Pocket door hardware		

Material for interior accessory shelf as required.

Note: All tops for this series of furniture are 1"-thick glued-up oak hardwood. All doors and drawer faces for this series of furniture are ¾"-thick particleboard shelving banded with ¾"-thick by ½"-wide oak hardwood.

Drawers Materials List

No.	Item	Dimensions T W L
4	Sides	½"x9½"x22"
2	Fronts	½"x9½"x29½"
2	Backs	½"x8¾"x29½"
2	Bottoms	¼"x21¾"x29½"
2	Drawer faces	¾"x11½"x32"
2	22" Drawer glide sets	

Step 1. Cut two ⅜"-deep by ¾"-wide rabbets on the inside back and bottom edge of each side panel. The panel also requires a ⅜"-deep by ¾"-wide dado, 24" up from the bottom edge.

PRO TIP

The easiest way to cut a rabbet or dado on a large sheet is to use a dado blade on the table saw.

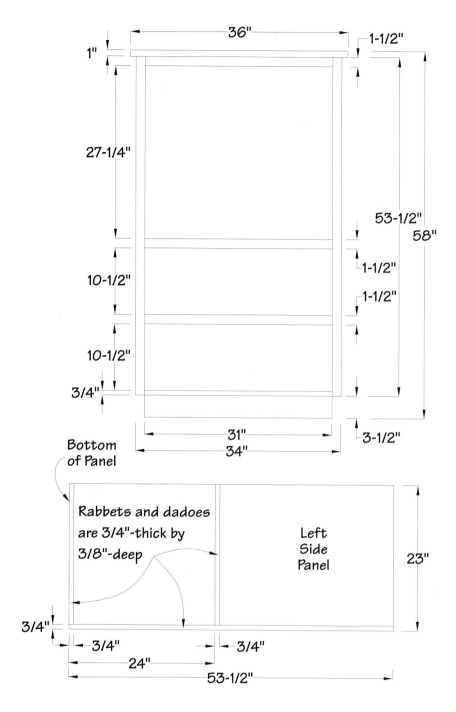

Rabbets and dadoes
are 3/4"-thick by
3/8"-deep

Bottom of Panel

Left
Side
Panel

Step 3. Install the bottom and middle fixed shelving. Add support cleats to the middle shelf to help support the television and other related equipment.

Step 5. Secure the rails with glue and screws through the stiles. Use 2" finishing nails on the bottom and middle shelf rails.

Step 4. Attach the Stiles

Cut two stiles (vertical face-frame members) at ¾"x1½"x53½", and secure to the carcass with glue and 2" spiral finishing nails. Align the outside edge of the stile with the outside face of the cabinet side panel.

Step 5. Add the Rails

There are four rails ¾"-thick by 31"-wide. Three of the rails are 1½" high, while the bottom rail is ¾" high. Secure the rails in position, as shown in the drawing, with glue and 2" screws. Predrill and counterbore the screw holes through the stile,

and fill with wood plugs. You can also use 2" finishing nails, on the face of the rail and into the shelf, where the bottom and middle rails meet the shelves. Sand the face frame, and round over the outside edge of the two stiles and the outside edge of the bottom rail.

BUILDING THE CABINET BASE

This style of cabinet base will be used on the TV armoire, dresser, chest of drawers and night table projects. It's a simple support made from solid oak boards ¾"-wide by 3½"-high. The base is strong and provides toe-kick space as well as a recess at the cabinet back that will fit over most wall molding. This feature allows the cabinet to be placed tightly against a wall. The pieces are glued and screwed together. Use 2" wood screws and counterbore the holes, which are to be filled with wood plugs. The frame is attached to the cabinet bottom with screws from the interior.

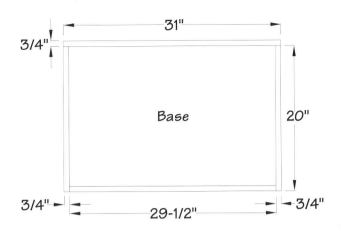

Step 6. Assemble the Base Frame

Cut the necessary pieces of wood. The outside dimension of the frame for the TV armoire is 20¾"-deep by 31"-wide. Draw a line around the bottom of the cabinet base board 1½" in from each edge. Set the square at 2¼" and draw another inner line. This will outline the base frame position.

Step 6. Draw the frame position on the base board at 1½" in from each edge.

Step 7. Install the Base Frame

Before attaching the base frame to the cabinet, drill small holes through the base cabinet in the middle of the frame outline. Space the holes about 6" apart. Next, apply glue to the frame and clamp it in place. The pencil outline will help you clamp it in position. Use the pilot holes that appear through the cabinet base as a guide to drill holes through the base board and into the frame. Install 2" wood screws in each hole, making sure the frame is drawn tightly against the underside of the base board.

Step 7. Attach the base frame with glue and 2" wood screws from the cabinet's interior.

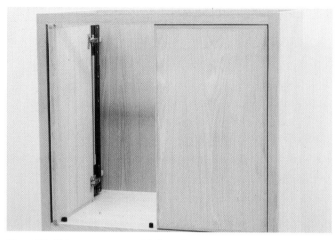

Step 8. Construct a door with ¾"-thick oak veneer particleboard shelving and ½"-wide by ¾"-thick hardwood edge strips.

Step 9B. Take your time and follow the steps carefully when installing the pocket door hardware.

Step 9A. Install 22" pocket door hardware as detailed in the manufacturer's instructions.

IMPORTANT!

This procedure of building a base frame and installing it on the cabinets will be used for all the previously mentioned cabinets. The only change will be the outside dimension of the frame. If the cabinet happens to be located over a floor heating register, a grill can be installed in the frame.

MAKING AND INSTALLING INSET DOORS

Step 8. Make the Doors

I will be using a hardwood-edged oak veneer particleboard door. The inset door needs clearance on its top and bottom edge. Therefore, the overall height of each door will be 27". The doors also need side and middle clearance, so cut them 15⅜" wide. That will provide a little

better than ¹⁄₁₆" clearance at each side and between the doors. Cut a ¾"-thick piece of oak veneer particleboard shelving, 14⅜"-wide by 26"-high. Next, cut two ¾"-thick hardwood strips ½"-wide by 26"-long and two at 15⅜" long. Attach the strips to the door edges with glue and brad nails, so the finished size of each door is 15⅜"-wide by 27"-high.

Note that this door-fabricating method will be identical for all the drawer faces in this chapter. The only difference will be the finished size.

Set the nails below the surface, and fill the holes with colored wood putty. Then, round over all the edges with a ¼" roundover router bit.

Step 9. Install the Pocket Door Hardware

I am using 22" pocket door hardware manufactured by Blum. The manufacturer supplies all the necessary installation instructions. I recommend you follow their procedures.

CONSTRUCTING THE TOP

The tops for the TV armoire, chest of drawers, dresser, night table, makeup desk and headboard projects are all made with 1"-thick oak. For more information about gluing up solid boards for panels see chapter nine, page 126. However, you can make the tops from any thickness wood you desire.

Step 10. Prepare the Top

Cut the top to a finished size of 25"-deep by 36"-wide. On the front and side edges, use a ⅜" roundover bit. Clamp the top in place, and mark where the inside face of the back board meets the top. Install a ¾"x1½"x32½" cleat on that line with glue and screws.

Step 11. Install the Top

Apply glue to the cabinet's top edges. Clamp the top in its proper location with a 1" overhang on the sides and a 1¼" overhang on the front edge. The top should be flush with the outside face of the back board. Predrill holes, and secure the top from the underside of the front rail and face of the rear cleat.

Step 12. Build the Accessory Shelf

The only additional accessory you will have to make is an interior shelf. The height is determined by the television you plan to use. My shelf is 9"-high by 26"-wide. The shelf is ¾"-thick particleboard with wood tape applied to the visible edges. Build the shelf 22" deep so wires and cables can be connected between the TV and any other equipment.

Step 10. Install a rear-mounting cleat on the underside of the top.

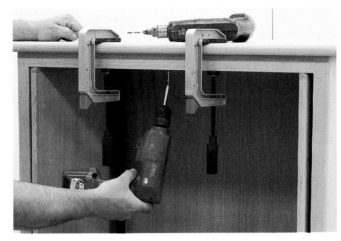

Step 11. Secure the top to the cabinet with glue and screws through the front rail and rear cleat previously attached to the top.

Step 12. Build a custom accessory shelf based on the television dimensions.

DRAWERS

The only item left to build is the drawer. Construction details will be found on the following page.

Skill Builder Building Birch Plywood Drawers With Bottom-Mounted Glides

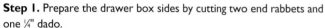

Step 1. Prepare the drawer box sides by cutting two end rabbets and one ¼" dado.

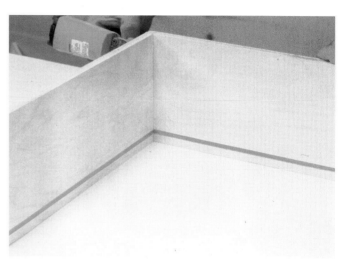

Step 3. Attach the front board to the sides with glue and nails.

All the projects in this chapter have drawers built of ½" cabinet grade plywood. You'll come across a few different names for this plywood, which is sometimes known as Baltic or Russian birch. But, no matter what it's called in your area, be sure it has "void-free" layers. Simply stated, all the layers should be free of holes or defects.

There are a couple of details to keep in mind when building this type of drawer. These dimensions are based on the Blum bottom-mounted drawer glides. The drawer box is 1" narrower than the opening and 1" less in height. The depth of the box equals the drawer-glide length. The drawer face is 1" wider than the opening and 1" greater in height. Check the specifications for your drawer glides.

BUILDING THE DRAWER BOX

I'll use the chest of drawers as an example for the stated dimensions.

The drawer glides are 16" bottom mounted. That drawer opening is 7¼"x17½"x33". Therefore, the drawer box size, when finished, will be 6¼"x16"x32".

Step 1. Make the Box Sides

Cut two sides ½"x6¼"x16". Each side will have a ½"-wide by ¼"-deep rabbet on both ends. The sides will also need a ¼"-wide by ¼"-deep dado with its top edge ¾" up from the bottom.

Step 2. Cut the Front and Rear Boards

Cut a front board ½"x6¼"x31½". It has to receive a ¼"-deep by ¼"-wide dado with the top edge ¾" up from the bottom.

The back board is ½"x5½"x31½". No dadoes or rabbets are required.

Step 3. Attach the Side and Front Boards

Secure the front board to the sides, in the dadoes, using glue and brad nails. Make certain the dadoes are aligned.

Step 4. Install the Back Board

Attach the back board by securing it with glue and brad nails in the rear side board rabbets.

Align the back board top edge with the side board top edges, making sure not to cover the dadoes.

Step 5. Build the Bottom Board

Cut a piece of birch plywood to ¼"x15¾"x31½". Slide it into the dado slots, which should place it flush with the back end of the back board. Secure it to the back board edge with brad nails. Do not use glue anywhere on this board.

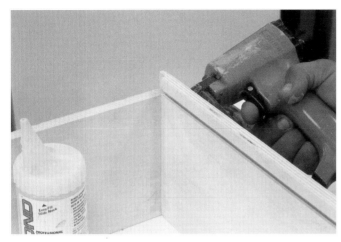

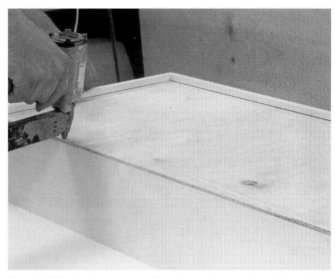

Step 4. Install the back board with glue and brad nails in the side rabbets. Place the drawer box upside down on a flat surface, so the top edges of all boards are even.

Step 5. Slide the bottom board into the dadoes, and attach it to the back board with brad nails.

Step 6. Install the Drawer Glides

Install the glides on the drawer box according to the manufacturer's instructions.

For our face-frame application, we must install ¾"-thick by 1½"-wide wood cleats to carry the carcass glide members straight back from the stile edge.

Step 7. Construct the Drawer Face

Construct a drawer face from ¾" oak veneer particleboard shelving and solid-wood strips, as detailed on page 92. Secure it to the box with four 1" screws from the inside. The drawer face should overlap the opening by ½" on the top, bottom and sides. For this example our drawer face is ¾"x8¼"x34".

Step 6. Attach the drawer glide set to the box and cabinet carcass.

Step 7. Attach the drawer face to the drawer box with 1" screws.

High-Capacity Dresser

There never seems to be enough drawer space in many of today's dressers. We're always looking for more room to store socks, undergarments, sweaters and T-shirts. This dresser project may be the answer to your needs. It's all drawers! Six wide, large-capacity drawers in a dresser that's more than 5' long. The style of this dresser project matches all the other furniture in this chapter. You can make all of them as a set or any one as a stand-alone unit. The choice is yours.

Materials List

The back and bottom boards are unveneered ¾"-thick particleboard shelving. They aren't visible, and plain particleboard is not as costly as the veneer-covered particleboard. The sides and middle vertical-divider boards are ¾" oak veneer particleboard shelving.

No.	Item	Dimensions T W L	Materials
2	Sides	¾"x17½"x25½"	Oak veneer particleboard
1	Center panel	¾"x17⅛"x25⅛"	Oak veneer particleboard
1	Back board	¾"x24¾"x64¼"	Particleboard shelving
1	Bottom board	¾"x17½"x64¼"	Particleboard shelving
2	Stiles	¾"x1½"x25½"	Oak
1	Bottom rail	¾"x¾"x62"	Oak
1	Top rail	¾"x1½"x62"	Oak
1	Center stile	¾"x1½"x23¼"	Oak
2	Middle rails	¾"x1½"x62"	Oak
1	Top	1"x19¼"x67"	Oak

Drawer Faces

All drawer faces are edged-oak particleboard shelving.

No.	Item	Dimensions T W L
4	Faces	¾"x7"x31¼"
2	Faces	¾"x9¼"x31¼"

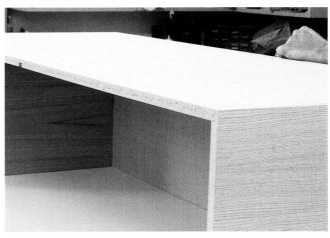

Step 2. Attach the bottom panel to the sides with glue and finishing nails.

Step 3. Attach the back to the side and bottom boards with glue and finishing nails.

Step 1. Cut the Carcass Panels

Cut the two sides, bottom, back and center panel as detailed in the materials list. All the panels, with the exception of the center panel, must receive ¾"-wide by ⅜"-deep dadoes and rabbets as shown in the drawing on page 98.

Step 2. Connect the Bottom and Side Panels

Place the bottom board in each side-panel bottom rabbet. Use glue and 2" spiral finishing nails that are driven through the bottom panel into the edge of the side panel. Verify that the bottom panel's dado is facing the cabinet interior.

Step 3. Install the Back

Place the back board in the side-panel rabbets, making sure it rests tightly against the bottom board. Use glue and finishing nails through the back board, into the sides, to secure the back. Nails should also be driven from the underside of the bottom board into the back board edge.

Step 4. Glue and nail the center panel in the back and bottom board dadoes.

Base Frame

All pieces are ¾"-thick by 3½"-high oak.

No.	Item	Dimensions T W L
1	Front	¾"x3½"x62"
2	Sides	¾"x3½"x14½"
1	Rear	¾"x3½"x60½"

Drawer Boxes

The drawer box sides, front and back boards are ½"-thick Baltic birch plywood. The bottom is ¼"-thick birch plywood.

No.	Item	Dimensions T W L
8	Sides	½"x5"x16"
4	Fronts	½"x5"x28¾"
4	Backs	½"x4¼"x28¾"
4	Sides	½"x7¼"x16"
2	Fronts	½"x7¼"x28¾"
2	Backs	½"x7¼"x28¾"
6	Bottoms	¼"x28¾"x15¾"
24	Shelf pins	½" diameter x 1½"

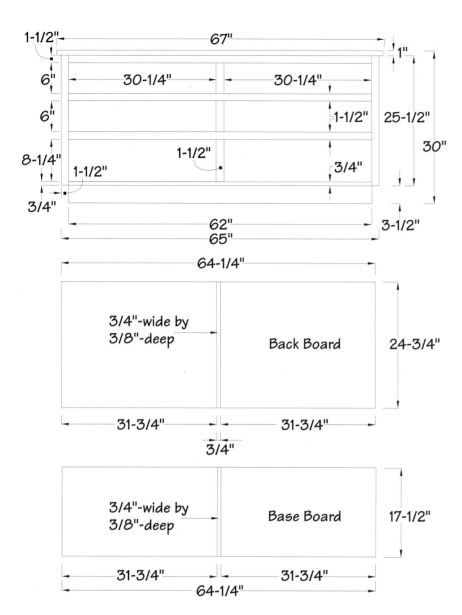

Step 5. Secure the two end stiles with glue and finishing nails.

Step 4. Attach the Center Panel

The center panel is placed in the aligned dadoes on the back and bottom boards. Brush glue in the dadoes, then drive and secure the panel with finishing nails through both back and bottom boards.

Step 5. Install the Stiles

Cut two stiles at ¾"x1½"x25½". Attach them to the outside edges of the cabinet with glue and finishing nails. The nail holes are filled with a colored putty stick matching the final finish. Verify that the outside edges of the stiles are flush with the outside edge of the cabinet.

Step 6. Install the Bottom Rail

Cut and install a ¾"x¾"x62" bottom rail to the cabinet. This rail should cover the bottom board's edge completely.

Step 7. Install the Top Rail

The top rail is ¾"x1½"x62". Secure the stiles to the top rail with glue and 2" wood screws in counter-bored pilot holes (which will be filled with wood plugs). Glue the center panel to the rail and secure with a finishing nail through the rail face. Before nailing, verify that the center panel is correctly positioned. The distance from center panel to end panel should be equal on the top and bottom.

Step 8. Prepare the Center Stile

The center stile is ¾"x1½"x23¼". Two dadoes are cut in the stile, as shown in the drawing. These will form a half-lap joint with the two middle rails. The center stile is attached to the center panel with the dadoes facing out. Verify that there is equal spacing between the center stile and the two outside stiles.

Step 6. Attach the bottom rail with glue and finishing nails.

Step 8. Cut two dadoes in the center stile.

Step 7. Install the top rail with screws through the stiles and then nailing into the center panel.

Step 9. Cut a dado in each middle rail, so a half-lap joint is formed with the center stile.

Step 9. Attach the Middle Rails

Cut two middle rails at ¾"x1½"x62". Both rails require a ⅜"-deep by 1½"-wide dado so they will lock with the middle stile forming half-lap joints. Secure the rails with glue and screws through the stiles at either end of the cabinet, as well as nails through the half-lap joint.

 PRO TIP

Temporarily place the middle rails in their correct positions. Use the center stile as a guide, and mark the dado location on the rail. It's more accurate than using a tape measure.

Step 10. Install a base frame on the cabinet.

Step 11. Install countertop clips, and apply glue to the cabinet's upper edge before installing the top.

Step 12. Use glue and ⅝" wood screws through the countertop clips to secure the cabinet top.

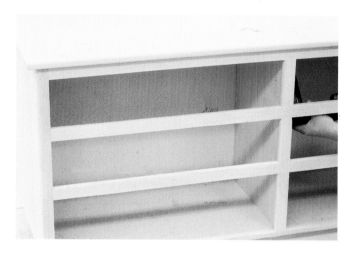

Step 10. Build the Base

Build a base using ¾"-thick by 3½"-high oak boards. The outside dimension should be 15¼"-deep by 62"-wide. See page 91 for installation procedures.

Step 11. Prepare to Install the Cabinet Top

Install countertop clips around the inside perimeter of the cabinet. Place four clips on the back and front, as well as two on each end. Glue up a top that's 1"x19¼"x67". See chapter nine, page 126, for procedures on board glue-ups. Apply glue on the upper edge of the cabinet in preparation for top installation.

Step 12. Install the Top

Round over the top and bottom edges on the front and two sides of the cabinet top. Place it on the dresser so there is a 1" overhang on the sides and front edge. Use ⅝" wood screws, inserted through the holes in the countertop clips, to secure the top.

BUILDING THE DRESSER DRAWERS

Build four upper drawers that are 5"x16"x29¼". The two bottom drawers are 7¼"x16"x29¼". The drawer fronts are ¾" thick, and you'll need four 7"-high by 31¼"-wide and two that are 9¼"-high by 31¼"-wide. Follow the assembly and installation instructions beginning on page 94. Perform a final sanding, and apply your favorite finish. Like all the projects in this chapter, the dresser was finished with three coats of oil-based semigloss polyurethane.

Chest of Drawers

This chest of drawers is another high-capacity storage unit. I've found it to be a great addition to our bedroom. There is plenty of wide, deep storage space for jeans and other casual clothes. It's built in the same style as the dresser. It's almost the same project with one exception. The center board on this project only divides the two top drawers and is therefore installed a little differently. Have fun building this project; I know you'll enjoy it for years to come.

Step 1. Assemble the Cabinet Carcass

Join the sides to the back and bottom boards following the same assembly procedures as the dresser.

Step 2. Install the Stiles and Rails

Cut and install the stiles and rails detailed in the materials list. Their position is shown at left. Follow the same assembly procedures for the dresser. Round over the outside edges of the stiles and bottom rail with a ⅜" roundover bit.

Step 3. Make the Center Stile

Cut the center stile, then plow a dado in the backside center of the stile at ⅜"-deep by ¾"-wide.

Step 2. Install the stiles and rails, as detailed in the drawings on page 102 and the photo at right.

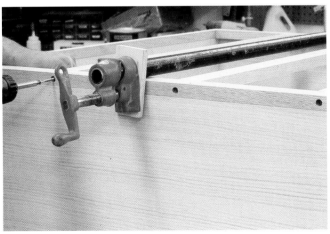

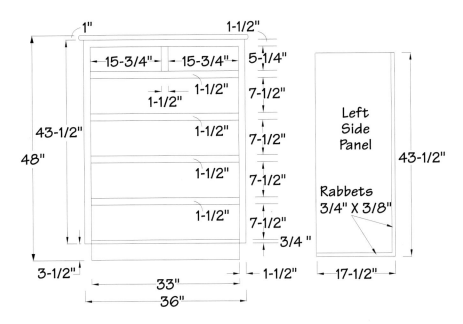

Materials List

Since they aren't visible, the back and bottom boards are of inexpensive unveneered ¾"-thick particleboard shelving. The sides and middle vertical divider boards are ¾" oak veneer particleboard shelving.

No.	Item	Dimensions T W L	Materials
2	Sides	¾"x17½"x43½"	Particleboard shelving
1	Center panel	¾"x5¼"x17⅛"	Particleboard shelving
1	Back board	¾"x42¾"x35¼"	Particleboard shelving
1	Bottom board	¾"x17½"x35¼"	Particleboard shelving
2	Stiles	¾"x1½"x43½"	Oak
1	Bottom rail	¾"x¾"x33"	Oak
1	Top rail	¾"x1½"x33"	Oak
1	Center stile	¾"x1½"x5¼"	Oak
4	Middle rails	¾"x1½"x33"	Oak
1	Top	1"x19¼"x38"	Oak

Drawer Boxes

The drawer box sides, front, and back boards are ½"-thick Baltic birch plywood. The bottom is ¼"-thick birch plywood.

No.	Item	Dimensions T W L
4	Sides	½"x4¼"x16"
2	Fronts	½"x4¼"x14¼"
2	Backs	½"x3½"x14¼"
2	Bottoms	¼"x14¼"x15¾"
8	Sides	½"x6½"x16"
4	Fronts	½"x6½"x31½"
4	Backs	½"x5¾"x31½"
4	Bottoms	¼"x15¾"x31½"

Step 4. Attach the Center Panel

Position the short center stile as shown at left. It's secured with glue and screws through the two adjoining rails. Cut the 17⅛"-long center panel from veneer stock. Place the center panel in the stile dado, and space the back end equally between the two side boards. Apply glue to both ends of the center panel, and secure the back end with screws through the back board. Clamp the center board in place until the glue sets.

Step 5. Install the Base

Build a base frame from ¾"-thick by 3½"-wide stock that measures 33"-wide by 15¼"-deep. Refer to page 91 for assembly and installation details.

Step 6. Install the Top

Install three countertop clips on the inside front and back of the cabinet and two on each end. Use ⅝" wood screws to secure the clips. Glue up and cut a wood top to a finished size of 1"x19¼"x38". This gives you a 1" overhang on the front and two sides. Apply glue to the top edges of the cabinet, and secure the top in place.

Step 7. Build the Drawers

Use the dimensions supplied in the materials list for all the drawer components. Cut all the pieces, and follow the assembly instructions on page 94 to complete the drawer installation.

After completing the chest, sand and apply the finish of your choice. I applied three coats of oil-based polyurethane to my chest of drawers.

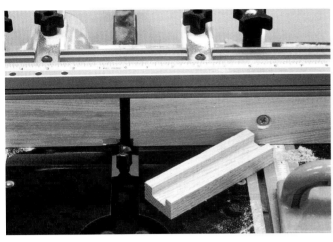

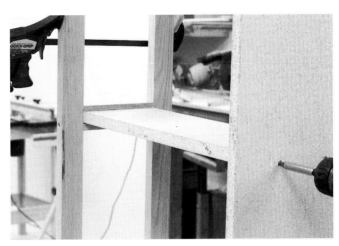

Step 3. Prepare a center stile, and cut a ¾"-wide by ⅜"-deep dado on the back side.

Step 4. Install the center stile and panel.

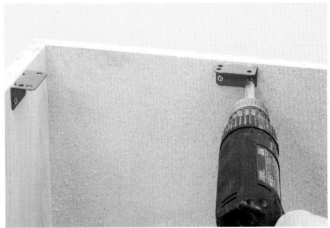

Step 5. Build and install a base frame that is set back 1½" from all edges.

Step 6. Install countertop clips prior to attaching the top.

Base Frame
All pieces are ¾"-thick by 3½"-high oak.

No.	Item	Dimensions T W L
1	Front	¾"x3½"x33"
2	Sides	¾"x3½"x14½"
1	Rear	¾"x3½"x31½"

Drawer Faces
All drawer faces are edged-oak particleboard shelving.

No.	Item	Dimensions T W L
2	Faces	¾"x6¼"x16¾"
4	Faces	¾"x8½"x34"

PRO TIP

There's always a wall plug right where a cabinet will be placed against the wall. It must be a subset of Murphy's Law. If you encounter this situation, cut a hole in the back board to give the plug a recess in the back of the cabinet. You'll then be able to push your cabinet tightly against the wall.

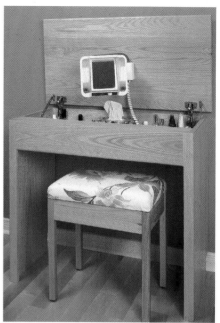

Makeup Desk and Bench

If you have three feet of spare wall space in your bedroom, this project is well worth considering. It can be used as a standard writing desk and has a storage compartment under the top that's perfect for cosmetics. The bench is a simple design with a particleboard seat meant to be padded and covered. Any material can be used to cover the bench; mine was chosen to match the room decor.

Materials List

Both the desk and bench have been built to match the other bedroom furniture in this project.

No.	Item	Dimensions T W L	Materials
Desk			
2	Sides	¾"x16¼"x29"	Oak veneer particleboard
2	Rails	¾"x4"x32½"	Oak veneer particleboard
2	Edge strips	¼"x¾"x32½"	Oak
2	Edge strips	¼"x¾"x16¼"	Oak
1	Elbow rest	¾"x2½"x32½"	Oak
1	Bottom board	¾"x16¼"x32½"	Oak particleboard
2	Face stiles	¾"x1½"x29¼"	Oak
1	Face rail	¾"x5¼"x31"	Oak
1	Top	1"x18"x36"	Oak
Bench			
4	Legs	1¼"x1¼"x17"	Oak
4	Stretchers	¾"x3½"x16"	Oak
1	Seat	¾"x12"x18"	Particleboard shelving

Step 3. Attach the rails to the side panels as shown.

Step 4. Secure the bottom board with glue and 2" wood screws.

BUILDING THE DESK

Step 1. Cut the Desk Sides

The desk sides are two pieces of ¾"-thick oak veneer particleboard shelving. Cut them 16¼"-deep by 29"-high.

Step 2. Cut the Desk Rails

The rails are made from ¾"-thick oak veneer particleboard shelving and are 4"-high by 32½"-wide.

Step 3. Assemble the Sides

Work with the desk turned upside down on a flat surface. Attach the sides to the rails so the tops are flush. Use glue and 2" screws through the sides. Plug the holes with wood plugs. Verify that both rails are flush with the outside edge of the side boards.

Step 4. Install the Bottom Board

Cut the ¾" oak veneer bottom board 16¼"-deep by 32½"-wide. Use glue and three 2" wood screws per edge to fasten the bottom board to the underside of the rails.

Step 5. Apply ¼"-thick hardwood edge strips to the desk's top edge. These strips will cover the exposed particleboard edge.

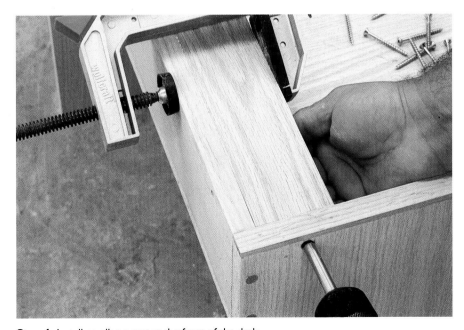

Step 6. Install an elbow rest at the front of the desk.

Step 7. Install the face-frame stiles and face rail on the front of the desk.

Step 8. Fill the nail holes, insert the necessary wood plugs, and sand.

Step 9. Install the desk top using 170° hidden hinges.

Step 5. Edge the Sides and Rails

Cut the wood edge strips to the specified dimensions. Secure them to the top edges of the sides and rails with glue and brad nails.

Step 6. Create an Elbow Rest

Cut a piece of solid oak that is ¾"x2½"x32½". Attach it flush with the front rail's top edge. It should be tightly drawn against the rail as shown. Use glue and screws from the side and front. The screw holes at the side will be filled with wood plugs. However, the screws through the front of the rail will be covered by another board.

Step 7. Add a Three-Sided Face Frame

Cut two face stiles and one face rail to the dimensions detailed in the materials list. Turn the desk on its back, and secure the stiles to the side edges with glue and finishing nails through the face. Both stiles are installed flush with the side boards' outer surface. Install the face rail on the front of the desk with it's top edge flush with both upper stile ends. Use 2" wood

Step 10. Cut the legs to size, and create the adjacent mortises on each bench leg.

Step 11. Cut the stretchers to length, and form a tenon on each end that is ⅜"x⅜"x3". Round over the tenon corners at the bottom so they will fit in the mortise.

Step 12. Assemble the bench using glue and clamps. Pin the joints with brad nails.

screws through the stile end to secure the rail. You can also drive three 1¼" wood screws from the inside of the desk into the rail.

Step 8. Complete the Face Frame

Sand and round over the inside and outside edges of the stiles, as well as the bottom edge of the rail, with a ⅜" roundover bit. Fill the nail holes, and sand the desk.

Step 9. Build the Desktop

Build the top to the dimensions shown in the materials list. Round over the top and bottom edge of the two sides and front. Install 170° hidden hinges. The hinges are mounted in the same manner as a cabinet door. For more details, see chapter four, page 52.

BUILDING THE BENCH

Step 10. Prepare the Legs

Use a router or router table to cut ⅜"x⅜"x3" mortises on two adjacent sides of each leg.

Step 14. Cut a piece of particleboard shelving for the top. Secure with screws through the corner blocks. Option: Make your bench top with 1" solid oak to match the desktop.

Step 11. Cut the Stretcher Tenons

Each stretcher requires a tenon on at both ends that is ⅜"x⅜"x3".

Step 12. Assemble the Bench

Join the four legs and stretchers. Use glue and clamp the bench until the glue sets, or pin the joints with a brad nail.

Step 13. Install Corner Blocks

Glue and screw right-angled corner blocks at each corner of the bench for added strength.

Step 14. Adding a Bench Top

Since the bench top is going to be covered with foam and material, any wood can be used. The particleboard top is ¾"x12"x18". It is fixed to the bench frame with screws through the corner blocks.

Bedside Cabinet/Bookcase

This combination night table and bookcase is part of the master bedroom storage-furniture suite. It has the same style base and top. The night table is a great addition to the bed project and, with two large-capacity drawers, provides extra storage. To take advantage of the often-unused space above the night table, I've added an upper section with adjustable shelves for even more storage. The sides will receive a bottom, top and back board using the same construction methods as the dresser and chest of drawers.

Step 1. Prepare the Side Panels

Cut the side panels, as illustrated in the drawing. The panels will require a rabbet that's ⅜"-deep by ¾"-wide on the top, back and bottom edges.

Step 2. Build the Cabinet Carcass

Attach the top, back and bottom boards to the side panels with glue and spiral finishing nails. Drive the nails from the back of each board into the edges of the side panel. Follow the same procedures as detailed for the dresser and chest-of-drawers assemblies.

Step 3. Drill Shelf Pin Holes

Make a shelf hole jig with 2" spaced guide holes. Clamp it in place and drill the holes.

Step 3. Make a shelf hole jig to accurately drill the holes for adjustable shelving.

 **PRO TIP**

Use the table saw to cut the reduced-width upper vertical section of the side panels to get a straight cut. Slowly approach the end of the cut and turn off the saw. Remove the side, and repeat the procedures for the horizontal or crosscut. Score the outside of the uncut portion with a knife, and complete the cut with a hand saw.

Step 4. Add Countertop Clips

Install three right-angle metal brackets per side. These will be used to secure the cabinet tabletop.

Step 5. Attach the Lower Face Frame

Install the lower section stiles and three rails. Follow the same procedures as the dresser face-frame installation, using glue and finishing nails. Round over the outside edges of the stiles and bottom rail.

Step 6. Build the Base Frame

Construct a base frame using the dimensions supplied in the materials list. Refer to page 91 for installation instructions.

Step 7. Form the Tabletop

Glue up a tabletop using 1"-thick material that's 18¼"-deep by 26"-wide. Cut out a notch on both sides of the top so it will fit tight against both cabinet sides and the back board.

Round over the top and bottom edges of the front and sides with a ⅜" roundover bit. Do not round over the notched area or the back edge.

Materials List			
No.	Item	Dimensions T W L	Materials
2	Sides	¾"x17¼"x70"	Oak particleboard
1	Bookcase top	¾"x7¼"x23¼"	Oak particleboard
1	Bottom	¾"x17¼"x23¼"	Oak particleboard
1	Back	¾"x23¼"x68½"	Oak particleboard
2	Lower stiles	¾"x1½"x24"	Oak
1	Bottom rail	¾"x¾"x21"	Oak
2	Lower rails	¾"x1½"x21"	Oak
1	Cabinet top	1"x18¼"x26"	Oak
2	Upper stiles	¾"x1½"x45"	Oak
1	Upper rail	¾"x1½"x21"	Oak
3	Shelves	¾"x6⅜"x22⅜"	Oak particleboard
Base Frame			
1	Front	¾"x3½"x21"	Oak
2	Sides	¾"x3½"x14¼"	Oak
1	Back	¾"x3½"x19½"	Oak
Drawers			
4	Sides	½"x9⅛"x16"	Baltic birch plywood
2	Fronts	½"x9⅛"x19½"	Baltic birch plywood
2	Backs	½"x8⅜"x19½"	Baltic birch plywood
2	Bottoms	¼"x15¾"x19½"	Baltic birch plywood
2	Drawer faces	¾"x11⅛"x22"	Oak particleboard
4	Edge strips	½"x¾"x12⅛"	Oak
4	Edge strips	½"x¾"x23"	Oak

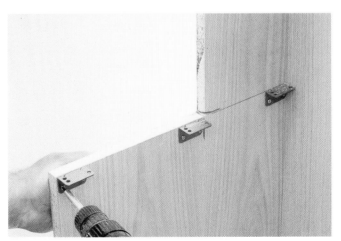

Step 4. Install the right-angle brackets to secure the cabinet top.

Step 8. Attach the Upper-Section Face Frame

Attach the upper-section stiles and rail. Round over the inner and outer edges of the frame with a ⅜" bit.

Step 9. Add Adjustable Shelves

Cut the shelves to size, as indicated in the materials list. Apply a wood edge veneer to the front edge, and test fit.

Step 5. Attach the lower-section stiles and rails. Round over the outside edge of the stiles and bottom rail with a ⅜" roundover bit.

Step 6. Attach the base frame to the cabinet bottom.

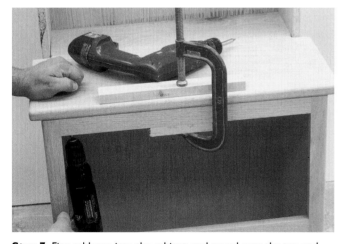

Step 7. Fit a tabletop into the cabinet, and round over the top and bottom exposed edges. Secure the top with glue and screws in the right-angle brackets.

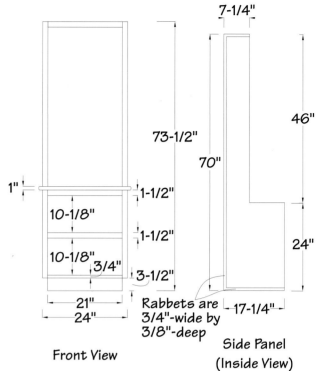

73-1/2"

10-1/8"

10-1/8"

1"

1-1/2"

1-1/2"

3/4"

3-1/2"

21"

24"

Rabbets are
3/4"-wide by
3/8"-deep

Front View

7-1/4"

46"

70"

24"

17-1/4"

**Side Panel
(Inside View)**

Night table/bookcase.

Step 8. Install the upper face frame. Round over the edges.

Step 10. Build the Drawers

Cut the drawer parts to size as shown in the materials list. Build the drawers following instructions detailed on page 94. Attach the drawer faces, and install the drawers, with 16" bottom-mounted drawer glides, in the cabinet.

Headboard With Hidden Storage

If you plan to add a headboard to the platform bed project in this chapter, then you may want to consider this version. It's a decorative finishing touch to the bed and is equipped with a hidden compartment. I've made my headboard shallow, but you can increase the storage compartment size for any special requirements. The headboard is made from oak veneer particleboard shelving and oak hardwood in a style that matches the other projects in this chapter.

Step 1. Attach the Front to the Side Boards

Cut the front board and apply wood veneer to the top edge. Attach the two 3½"-wide by 32"-long side boards to the front panel with glue and screws. The sides of my headboard will be hidden by the night tables I've built, so it isn't necessary to counterbore and fill the screw holes. If your sides will be exposed, fill the holes with wood plugs.

Materials List

All material is ¾"-thick oak particleboard shelving or oak hardwood. The top is 1" thick.

No.	Item	Dimensions T W L	Materials
1	Front	¾"x32"x78½"	Oak particleboard shelving
1	Back	¾"x15"x80"	Oak particleboard shelving
2	Sides	¾"x3½"x32"	Oak
1	Bottom	¾"x3½"x78½"	Oak
1	Top	1"x5¼"x80"	Oak

Step 1. Glue and screw the sides to the front board.

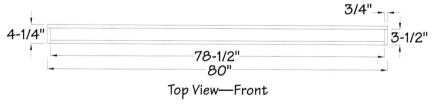

Top View—Front

Top view of headboard.

Step 2. Install the back panel with glue and 1½" wood screws. If the sides will be visible, apply wood veneer tape to the back board ends.

Step 3. Install the bottom board using right-angle brackets.

Step 2. Add a Back Panel

Prior to installing the back panel, apply wood veneer tape to the top edge. Use glue and 1½" screws to secure the back to the edge boards.

Step 3. Install the Bottom Board

Cut a bottom board ¾"x3½"x78½". I used a solid piece of oak because it was convenient; however, you may decide to use oak veneer particle-board shelving. Secure the bottom board to the back board with screws. Use right-angle brackets to attach the bottom to the front panel as shown.

Step 4. Attach the Top Board

The last piece to be added is the headboard top. Mine is 1" thick to match the other bedroom furniture. It's 5¼"-deep by 80"-wide solid oak. Only the top and bottom front edges have been rounded over with a ⅜" roundover router bit.

The top is mounted with three Blum 107° hidden hinges. Follow the installation procedures for this hinge as detailed in chapter four, page 52.

Step 4. Install the top with hidden hinges.

Platform Bed With Storage Drawers

Here's a project that makes use of all the wasted space under our beds. When you consider that large beds take up almost 45 square feet of floor space, it's easy to understand why reclaiming that space is worthwhile. The bed is easy to build and is assembled so it can be partially dismantled if a move becomes necessary. It's a well-built piece of furniture suitable for any bedroom. This platform storage bed is designed to accommodate a king-size mattress. If you are using any other size, you will have to adjust the dimensions accordingly.

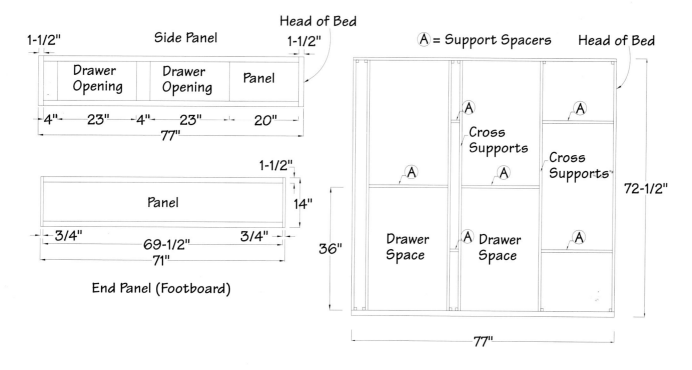

End Panel (Footboard)

Step 1. Build two side frames by joining the stiles to the rails using butt joints.

Materials List

I used ¾"-thick material including solid oak, oak veneer particleboard shelving, non-veneered particleboard shelving, and plywood.

No.	Item	Dimensions T W L	Materials
Base Material			
4	Side frame rails	¾"x1½"x77"	Oak
4	Side frame stiles	¾"x½"x14"	Oak
2	Side frame panels	¾"x11"x20"	Oak particleboard
4	Side frame panels	¾"x11"x4"	Oak particleboard
2	Footboard frame rails	¾"x1½"x69½"	Oak
2	Footboard frame stiles	¾"x¾"x14"	Oak
1	Footboard panel	¾"x11"x69½"	Oak particleboard
12	Side board cleats	¾"x¾"x14"	Oak
5	Cross supports	¾"x14"x71"	Particleboard
2	Support spacers	¾"x14"x20"	Particleboard
2	Support spacers	¾"x14"x23"	Particleboard
2	Support spacers	¾"x14"x2½"	Particleboard
Platform Material			
2	Platform side rails	¾"x5¼"x82"	Oak
2	Platform end rails	¾"x5¼"x78½"	Oak
2	Platform side cleats	¾"x¾"x80½"	Oak
2	Platform end cleats	¾"x¾"x77"	Oak
1	Platform center board	¾"x47"x78½"	Plywood
1	Platform center board	¾"x33½"x78½"	Plywood
Drawers and Drawer Faces			
8	Sides	½"x10"x30"	Baltic birch plywood
4	Fronts	½"x10"x21½"	Baltic birch plywood
4	Backs	½"x9¼"x21½"	Baltic birch plywood
4	Bottoms	¼"x29¾"x21½"	Baltic birch plywood
4	Drawer faces	¾"x12"x24"	Oak particleboard

Step 1. Build the Side Frames

Assemble the two side frames using two side frame rails and four side-frame stiles. Refer to the drawing. Join the stiles to the rails with glue and screws in counterbored holes using butt joints as shown.

Step 2. Build the Footboard

Assemble one footboard in the same manner, using two footboard rails and two rails. Notice that the footboard stiles are ¾" wide in comparison to the 1½"-wide sideboard stiles. Refer to the drawing.

Step 3. Install the Side and Footboard Panels

Cut the oak particleboard shelving panels for the side and footboards, as indicated in the materials list. Place the panels in their respective frames (see drawing). Use glue and 2" screws through the top and bottom rails to support the panels. Always drill pilot holes before inserting the screws.

Step 4. Install the Side Board Cleats

Each side board requires six ¾"-square by 14"-high cleats. They are attached with glue and 1¼" screws. Two cleats are installed ¾" back from each end. The remaining four cleats are attached ¾" back from each drawer opening.

🪚 PRO TIP

Use the joint you feel most comfortable with when building the frames. It's possible to use mortise and tenon, half-lap dado, dowels or biscuits. I'm using a butt joint to illustrate the basic method.

Step 5. Join the Sides and Footboard

Attach the sides to the footboard with three 1¼" screws through the cleats. Round over the outside corners with a ⅜" router bit.

Step 6. Secure the Cross Supports

The cross supports are secured with screws into the cleats. Position as shown in the drawing.

ASSEMBLY NOTE

From this point forward, use screws only when assembling sections so they can be dismantled if moving is necessary.

Step 3. Glue and screw the center panels for the side and foot boards.

Step 4. Attach the side board cleats with glue and 1¼" screws.

Step 5. Attach the sides to the footboard with 1¼" screws.

Step 6. Attach the cross supports. They will help support the mattress platform and provide a side wall where the drawer rails will be mounted.

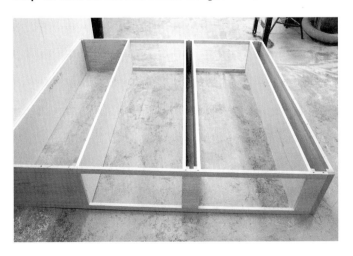

Step 7. Install the support spacers to minimize movement of the cross supports.

Step 9. Attach the platform support cleats on the inside of the frame.

Step 10. Install the platform center boards.

Step 7. Install Support Spacers

Install support spacers to minimize cross-support side movement for the drawer glides. The locations are not critical as long as the drawer-space supports are positioned in the middle of the drawer space.

BUILDING THE MATTRESS PLATFORM

Step 8. Build the Platform Frame

Join the two side rails to the end rails using glue and 2" wood screws. Plug the holes. The outside measurement of the finished frame should be 80"-wide by 82"-long.

Step 9. Attach Platform Cleats

Install the four platform cleats flush with the bottom edge of the mattress frame. Use glue and 1¼" wood screws at about 12" centers.

Step 10. Cut the Center Boards

Cut the two center boards for the mattress frame. Put the 47"-long sheet at the headboard end of the bed. That will position the joint over the center cross supports. Secure with 1¼" wood screws through the plywood and into the frame cleats. The platform is held to the base with four screws through the center panel and into the cross supports.

Position the head of the platform flush with the head of the base. Equally space the overhang on the sides and end.

Step 11. Build the Drawers

Use the dimensions supplied in the materials list. Refer to page 94 for instructions on drawer assembly and installation.

Children's Bedroom Storage Furniture

Pirate's Toy Chest

The projects in this chapter are made with #1 and #2 grade pine. These grades have quite a few knots and some surface defects but are inexpensive. Knotty pine is great for a style of furniture called "country pine" or "rustic furniture."

A child's toy box is where they keep all their worldly treasures, and it's an important part of growing up. It's their special place for the many things that have value to them. To add a little more importance and wonder to the toy box, I've created a "treasure chest" that roughly resembles a pirate chest of long ago. Many of the projects in this section use solid wood "glue-ups" as panels. I'll show you how to make your own panels later in this chapter.

BUILDING THE TOY CHEST

Step 1. Join the Panels

Glue up four panels as indicated in the materials list. For glue-up procedures, see page 126. Join the front and back panels to the sides with glue and 2" screws. Counterbore the pilot holes and fill with wood plugs. The finished outside dimension of the box should be 24½"-deep by 35"-wide.

Materials List

All the material used is ¾"-thick pine unless otherwise noted. Joining a number of boards together, as detailed on page 126, makes a panel.

No.	Item	Dimensions T W L
2	Side panels	¾"x20"x23"
2	Front and back panels	¾"x20"x35"
2	Bottom supports	¾"x2"x23"
2	Bottom supports	¾"x2"x32"
2	Base trim	¾"x2"x24½"
2	Base trim	¾"x2"x36½"
1	Bottom (plywood)	¾"x23"x33½"
3	Top supports (arc)	¾"x7¼"x24"
19	Top slats (angled)	¾"x1½" (approx.) x35"

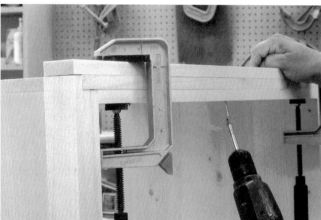

The first and last lid slats.

The middle slats.

Step 1. Attach the front and back panels to the sides with glue and 2" wood screws. Plug the holes, and sand smooth.

Step 2. Prepare Base Trim and Bottom Supports

Cut the four base trim pieces and the four bottom support boards to length. Secure the boards to the inside and outside of the box. Set all boards flush with the box's bottom edge. Secure with glue and screws from the inside of the box.

Step 3. Dress the Base Trim

Use a ¼" roundover bit to ease the top edge of the base trim.

Step 2. Install the bottom support boards and the base trim flush with the bottom of the chest. Use 2" screws from the inside of the box to secure the boards.

Step 3. Round over the top edge of the base trim.

Step 4. Add a Bottom Board

Cut a ¾"-thick piece of plywood 23"-wide by 33½"-long. Place it in the chest, resting on the bottom support boards. Secure with glue and 1½" wood screws.

Step 5. Make Arc Lid Supports

On a board, draw an arc that is 23" wide and 7" high in the center. I use a stick to make a marking gauge to create my arc. The fixed, or nail, point of the gauge was set 13" in line and back from the 7"-high mark on my board. Therefore, my arc was 23" at its widest point and 7" high at the center, or 11½", mark. Cut the arc with a jigsaw or band saw, and

Step 5. Cut three arcs for the chest lid.

Step 6. Attach three slats on the front and back before removing the assembly and attaching the center arc.

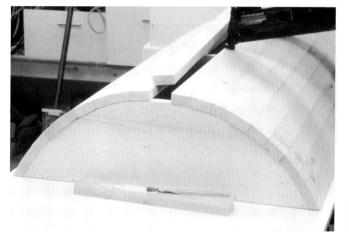

Step 7. The top, or last slat, may require a slight correction for a perfect fit.

Step 8. Install self-balancing lid support to prevent the lid from closing too fast.

use it as a pattern to create two additional arcs.

Note: Test fit three or four slats before cutting all of them. Drawing, cutting and sanding the arcs may produce a slightly different radius than mine.

Step 6. Install the Lid Slats

Refer to the drawings on page 118, then cut the slats. Don't cut the 19th (top middle) slat until the others are installed. You may need to adjust it slightly. Mine was 1⅝" wide with 3° angled cuts on both sides.

Clamp the two end arcs in place on the box, and install the first and last slats. The 30° side of these slats rests against the box. Install the slat boards from each side working towards the middle. Secure three slats on each side, remove the lid, set it on a flat surface and install the middle arc. Continue installing the slats using glue and finishing nails through the top of the slat into each arc.

Step 7. Complete Slat Installation

Measure, cut and install the last slat. Sand the ends and top of the lid so all slats are even. Be sure to sand the first and last slats flush with the front and back panels.

PRO TIP

After cutting the arcs, clamp them securely together. Sand all three until the arc is smooth. This way the three will be identical. Maintain their front and back relationships when attaching slats.

Step 8. Install the Hardware

Install a self-balancing lid support to keep the lid from slamming shut on fingers. I installed black 3" butt hinges and black handles (in the outdoor fence section of home stores) to give it an antique appearance. Finish the chest with three coats of oil-based polyurethane.

Rustic Pine Chest of Drawers

This rustic pine chest is easy to build. With five large drawers it can hold a great deal of clothing. The chest is a low-cost solution to organizing a child's bedroom. But don't stop with the chest—it's only the beginning. You can easily build a matching dresser and armoire in the same style by altering a few dimensions. Traditional, country or rustic pine furniture is simplicity at its best. The drawers are solid wood with an applied drawer front. They slide on wood frames that—with a little paste wax applied once a year—work very well. No fancy hardware here, just solid wood. The top and sides are glued-up ¾"-thick pine boards. The techniques for creating these panels are described in this chapter. I'm using #1 and #2 pine, which is fairly inexpensive.

Step 3. Join the frames using glue on each tenon. Pin the joint with two brad nails.

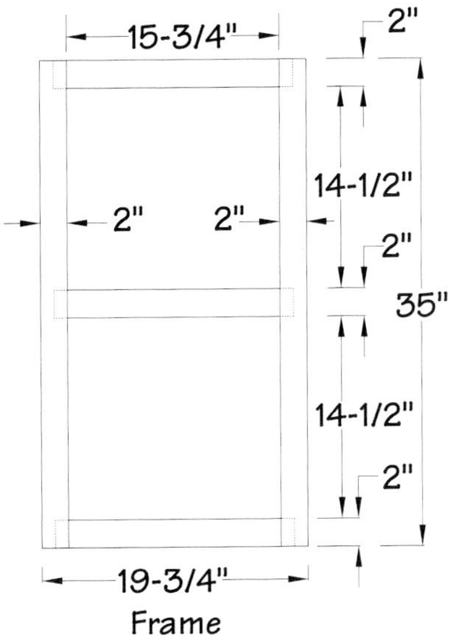

The cabinet frame.

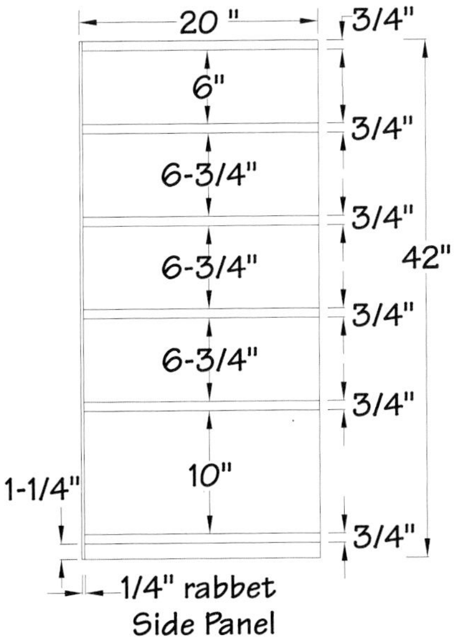

Dado and rabbet placement on side panels.

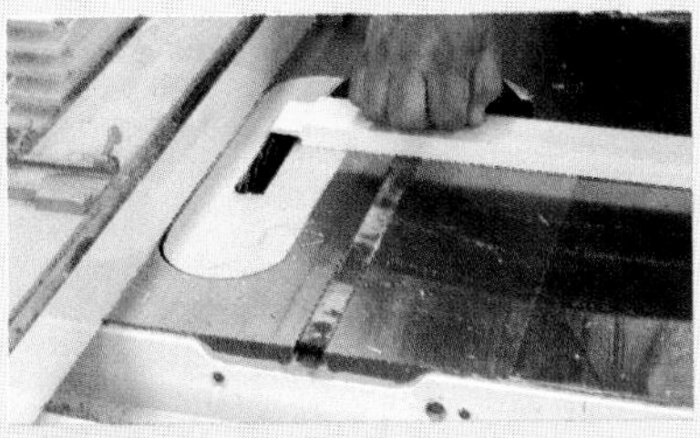

PRO TIP

Tenons are easily cut with a dado blade on a table saw.

Materials List

All materials are ¾"-thick pine with the exception of the back board.

No.	Item	Dimensions T W L
2	Sides	¾"x20"x42"
12	Frame members	¾"x2"x35"
18	Frame members	¾"x2"x17¾"
1	Back board	¼"x35"x41"
1	Front base board	¾"x3"x37½"
2	Side base boards	¾"x3"x20"
1	Top	¾"x21"x38"
1	Front base board cleat	¾"x1¼"x34½"
Drawers and Fronts		
2	Sides	¾"x5⅞"x19½"
1	Front	¾"x5⅞"x33⅜"
1	Back	¾"x5⅛"x33⅜"
1	Bottom	¼"x19"x33⅜"
1	Drawer face	¾"x6½"x35"
6	Sides	¾"x6⅝"x19½"
3	Fronts	¾"x6⅝"x33⅜"
3	Backs	¾"x5⅞"x33⅜"
3	Bottoms	¼"x19"x33⅜"
3	Drawer faces	¾"x7¼"x35"
2	Sides	¾"x9⅞"x19½"
1	Front	¾"x9⅞"x33⅜"
1	Back	¾"x9⅛"x33⅞"
1	Bottom	¼"x19"x33⅜"
1	Drawer face	¾"x10½"x35"

BUILDING THE CHEST CARCASS

Step 1. Prepare the Sides

Glue up and cut two side panels to a finished size of ¾"x20"x42". See page 126 for procedures on board glue-ups.

Step 2. Build the Frames

Cut the frame members as indicated in the materials list. The shorter members require a ¼"x1"x2" tenon on each end (see drawing of the cabinet frame above). The long members require a ¼"-wide by 1 1/16"-deep dado on one long edge.

Step 3. Assemble the Frames

Construct the frames as shown in the cabinet frame drawing. Apply glue to each tenon, and slide the tenon into the mortise. Secure the joint with two small brad nails until the glue sets.

Step 4. Prepare the Side Panels

Cut five ¼"-deep by ¾"-wide dadoes and one rabbet on each inside face of the side panels. Cut a ¼"-deep by ¼"-wide rabbet along one inside back edge to receive the back panel (see drawing at bottom left).

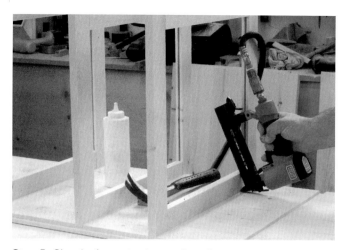

Step 5. Glue the frames in place, and pin the joint with a finishing nail.

Step 6. Install the ¼"-thick plywood cabinet back. Verify that the cabinet is square before completely nailing the back.

Step 5. Attach the Frames

Attach the frame assemblies to the chest sides. Use glue and small finishing nails to secure the frames. Frame members can be pinned in place by toe nailing. Be careful not to drive the nail through the side panel.

Step 6. Install the Back Board

Cut a piece of ¼"x35½"x41" plywood. This back board is glued and nailed into the rabbet on each side panel. Nail one side, then check that the cabinet is square by measuring the diagonals. Adjust if necessary, and complete the nailing.

Step 7. Cut the Base Boards

The base consists of three boards cut to the dimensions shown in the drawing on page 123. Cut and sand all boards.

Step 8. Install the Base Boards

Attach a ¾"x1¼"x34½" front baseboard support cleat under and at the front edge of the lower frame. Secure the base boards to the chest using glue and 1¼" screws from inside the chest carcass. Note that the 2¼" straight edges on the side

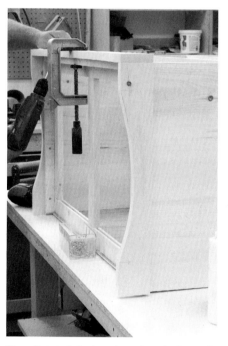

Step 8. Install the base boards with glue and 1¼" screws from the inside of the chest. Round over the top edge of the base board.

Step 9. Attach the top with 1¼" screws. It overhangs the front and sides of the chest by 1" and is flush with the back.

boards butt against the front base board. The ¾" thickness of the front board, when added to the side, provides a 3"-wide foot. The boards are installed 1½" up from the bottom edges of the sides. Round over the top edges of the base boards with a ¼" roundover bit. No router? Ease the edges with sandpaper.

Step 9. Attach the Top

Construct a glued-up panel as detailed on page 126. Cut a ¾"-thick top that is 21"-deep by 37¾"-wide. Round over the top and bottom edges of the front and sides with a ⅜" roundover bit. Secure the top with 1¼" screws through the top frame.

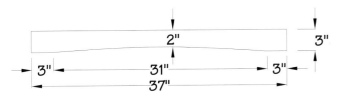

The base boards.

Front Base Board

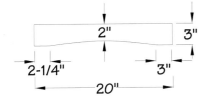

Side Base Board

PRO TIP

Accurate, well-defined dado and rabbet joints are easily accomplished on a table saw with a good-quality carbide dado blade.

Step 10. Build the Drawers

Cut the drawer parts according to the materials list. Refer to page 132 for details on building and installing rustic pine drawers.

OPTIONS

The chest of drawers shown above illustrates another example of the traditional building style. Instead of pine, I used red oak. The base design is accomplished by cutting a notch in the side panels. The front footboard is cut and attached to the bottom frame. However, the building style is identical to the rustic pine chest. To add interest, I divided the top drawer space by adding a vertical frame. This created space for two small drawers.

Rustic Pine Bedside Table

This rustic pine bedside table has been designed to complement the bed and chest projects in this chapter. It's a simple design with glued-up panels. The table has a storage drawer and lower shelf for books.

BUILDING THE BEDSIDE TABLE

Step 1. Prepare the Side Panels

Glue up two side panels and cut to a finished size of 18"-deep by 19¾"-high. See page 126 for glue-up details. Cut the dado and rabbet in each side. Attach the cleats with glue and 1¼" screws, as shown in the drawing on page 125.

Step 2. Join Sides to Bottom

Attach the two sides to the bottom board by securing it in the side dadoes. Use glue and 1½" screws from the outside. Plug the counter-bored screw holes with wood plugs.

Step 3. Attach Decorative Rails

Install the two rails with glue and finishing nails driven into the ends of the side panel cleats.

Step 4. Install the Back Board

Secure the back board in the side rabbets with glue and brad nails.

Step 5. Add the Top

Cut the top to ¼"x19"x23". Round over the top and bottom edges of the front and sides. Attach the top with glue and 1¼" screws, so it's flush with the cabinet back, with a 1" overhang on the front and sides. Attach screws from the underside.

No.	Item	Dimensions T W L
2	Sides	¾"x18"x19¼"
4	Cleats	¾"x1"x17"
1	Bottom shelf	¾"x17¾"x20"
2	Rails	¾"x¾"x19½"
1	Back	¼"x18"x20"
1	Top	¾"x19"x23"
1	Front base board cleat	¾"x1¼"x19½"
1	Front base board	¾"x3"x22½"
2	Side base boards	¾"x3"x18"
Drawer and Drawer Face		
2	Sides	¾"x5⅛"x17½"
1	Front	¾"x5⅛"x18⅜"
1	Back	¾"x4⅜"x18⅜"
1	Bottom	¾"x18⅜"x17"
1	Drawer face	¾"x5¾"x20"

Materials List
All the material is ¾"-thick pine with the exception of the back board.

Step 2. Attach the sides to the bottom board with glue and 1½" wood screws. The bottom board must be seated firmly in the dadoes.

Step 3. Attach the decorative rails to the ends of the side panel cleats with glue and nails.

Step 5. Attach the ¼" back board with brad nails. The top is secured with 1¼" screws, from the underside, through the side panel cleats.

Step 6. The front base board support cleat is attached to the underside of the bottom board with glue and screws.

Step 7. Install the base boards with glue and 1¼" screws.

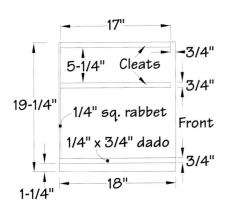

The side panel assembly.

17"
5-1/4" Cleats
3/4"
3/4"
19-1/4"
1/4" sq. rabbet
Front
1/4" x 3/4" dado
3/4"
1-1/4"
18"

Step 6. Add the Front Base Board Support Cleat

This cleat is needed to firmly attach the front base board. Use glue and 1½" screws in countersunk holes to secure the cleat.

Step 7. Add a Base Skirt

Cut the base boards to length. Form the arc by following the same procedures as used for the chest of drawers project on page 101. Attach the base skirt with glue and screws from the inside of the cabinet.

BUILDING THE DRAWERS

Refer to page 132 in this chapter for construction details on building rustic pine drawers.

Skill Builder   Creating Solid-Wood Panels

Step 1.

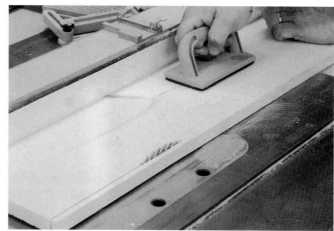

Step 2.

Step 3.

Successful panel glue-ups can be accomplished with your table saw. All that's needed is a well-tuned saw and a little care.

Step 1
First, make certain the table saw blade is sharp and the fence is parallel to the blade. The blade should be at a 90° angle to the top.

Step 2
Rip one edge of each board, then reverse, and rip the other edge.

Step 3
Line up the panels, making certain that they butt tightly together. If there is a gap, rip small amounts off each side until the board is straight.

Mark across two boards as a reference for the biscuit slots. If possible, alternate the growth rings on adjoining boards.

Step 4.

Step 5.

Step 6.

Step 4

Accurately cut the biscuit slots. Make certain the tool rests flat on the board surface.

Step 5

Apply an even coat of glue to both edges. Brush glue into the biscuit slots and insert the biscuits.

Step 6

Clamp the boards, alternating the clamps on the top and bottom. Tighten the clamps until the glue begins to squeeze out of the joint. Do not over tighten, as you will starve the joint of glue.

Step 7

Once the glue has set according to the manufacturer's specifications, scrape the joint of hard glue. Sand the panel, and cut to the required size.

Step 7.

Children's Storage Bed

This platform storage bed project is a great addition to any child's room. It features a bookcase headboard and four large storage drawers.

The bed is built of knotty pine, in the rustic or country style, to match the chest and night table projects. The dimensions given are to accommodate a mattress measuring 39"-wide by 75"-long.

I've also detailed a construction method using knock-down hardware. The cap bolts used here can be removed and replaced when the bed is moved.

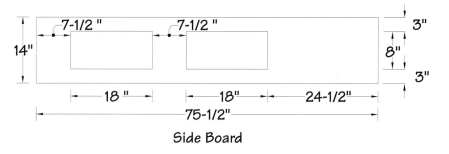

Side Board

The side panel cutouts.

BUILDING THE BASE

Step 1. Make the Panels

Form two side panels at 14"-high by 75½"-long and one footboard panel 14"-high by 36"-long. Refer to page 126 for details on making wood panels.

Step 2. Cut the Drawer Openings

Cut two openings in each side panel, as shown in the drawing at left. Score the outline with a knife to minimize edge damage, and cut the opening with a jigsaw.

Step 3. Install the Cross-Support Cleats

Make eight cleats that are 1½"-square by 14"-high. Screw and glue the blocks on the inside face of each side panel. They are secured to the sides, ¾" back from each drawer opening.

Step 3. Attach the cross-support cleats to the sides, ¾" back from each drawer opening.

Step 4. Attach the Corner Blocks

Attach the corner blocks to the inside face of each end board. The 2¼" face of the block is installed flush with the outside edge of each end panel.

Knockdown fasteners, called cap bolts, are used to join the side and end boards at each corner. These are easily removed and replaced if the bed has to been taken apart.

Step 5. Install the Cross Supports

Four ¾"x14"x36" cross supports will be used to strengthen the base and provide runners for the drawers.

Each cross support requires a 3"-high cleat on the top and bottom to form tracks for the drawers. Use glue and 1¼" screws to attach the boards.

Materials List		
All material is ¾"-thick knotty pine or plywood.		
No.	**Item**	**Dimensions T W L**
Base		
2	Frame sides	¾"x14"x75½"
2	End boards	¾"x14"x36"
4	Corner blocks	1½"x2¼"x14"
8	Cross support cleats	1½"x1½"x14"
4	Cross supports	¾"x14"x36"
8	Drawer cleats	¾"x3"x36"
Mattress Platform		
1	Plywood platform	¾"x40"x76"
2	Side boards	¾"x4¾"x77½"
2	End boards	¾"x4¾"x40"
Headboard		
2	Sides	¾"x7"x39¼"
1	Shelf	¾"x6¾"x40"
1	Top	¾"x8"x43½"
1	Back board	¼"x13"x40½"
1	Front panel	¾"x12"x40"
2	Lower front panels	¾"x7¼"x14½"
Drawers		
8	Sides	¾"x7⅞"x17"
4	Fronts	¾"x7⅞"x16⅞"
4	Backs	¾"x7⅛"x16⅞"
4	Bottoms	¾"x16½"x16⅞"
4	Drawer fronts	¾"x8½"x18½"

Step 4. Install the corner blocks, and secure the sides to the end boards with cap bolts.

Step 5. Attach the drawer cleats to the top and bottom edges of the cross supports.

Step 6. Install the cross supports in the base frame.

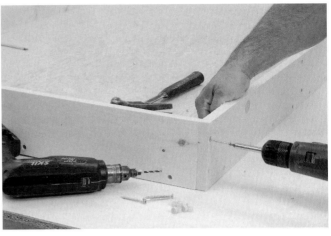

Step 7. Build a mattress platform by attaching the rails and end boards. Then use a router to round over the inner and outer top edges of the rails and end boards.

Step 8. Secure the mattress platform to the base with 2" screws. Do not use glue, so the frame can be removed.

Step 9. Attach the sides to the shelf 12" down from the top edge of the side panels.

Step 6. Attach the Cross Supports

Screw the cross-support assemblies to the support cleats with 2" screws. Do not glue these in place, so they can be removed when dismantling the bed. Notice that the drawer cleats face into each drawer space.

BUILDING THE MATTRESS PLATFORM

Step 7. Assemble the Platform

Cut the plywood, rails and sides for the platform, as detailed in the materials list.

Join the end boards to the plywood, and attach the rails. Use glue with 2" wood screws in counterbored holes. Fill with wood plugs.

The plywood sheet is attached flush with the bottom edge of the rails and end boards. The overall outside dimension of the frame is 41½"-wide by 77½"-long.

Step 8. Install the Platform

Secure the mattress platform to the base with 2" screws through the plywood into the corner blocks.

The headboard end of the frame is flush with the base. The sides and

footboard end should overhang the base by 2".

BUILDING THE HEADBOARD

Step 9. Cut the Parts

Cut all the headboard pieces, as detailed in the materials list. Before beginning the assembly, cut a ¼"-deep by ¼"-wide rabbet on the back inside edge of the two side boards.

Join the shelf to the sides, 12" down from the top edges, with glue and screws. Install the screws from the outside, and fill the counterbored holes with wood plugs.

Step 10. Cut a stopped rabbet on the underside rear of the top board. Attach the top with glue and screws so there is a 1" overhang on both ends.

Step 11. Attach the back board and front panel.

Step 10. Install the Top

Cut the top board, and round over the front and ends. Use a ¼" roundover bit on the top and bottom of each edge.

The top also requires a stopped rabbet that's ¼"-wide by ¼"-deep to receive the back board. A stopped rabbet is a common rabbet that stops 1" short of the board's ends. This will prevent the rabbet from being visible on the underside of the top.

Secure the top to the sides with glue and screws in plugged holes. Ensure the sides are spaced 40" apart and the top extends 1" past each side board.

Step 11. Attach the Front Panel and Back Board

Cut both the front panel and back board to size. Install the ¼" back board with glue and brad nails in the rabbet joint.

The front panel rests tight to the underside of the shelf. It is secured with glue and screws in plugged holes through the sides and shelf boards.

Step 12. Attach the lower front panels.

The front panel should be installed flush with the front edges of the sides and shelf boards.

Step 12. Attach the Lower Front Panels

Cut two lower front panels. They are needed to hide the space between the headboard sides and the base.

Join them flush with the side board front edge and tight to the front panel bottom edge.

Use screws and glue. I've also used a small wood block to support the lower and front panel joint. Install this block behind the joint using glue and screws.

Step 13. Building the Drawers

Cut all the drawer parts and refer to page 132 for assembly and installation details.

Skill Builder   Building Rustic Pine Drawers

The are many styles of drawer-mounting hardware available in today's marketplace. But, before all these great solutions existed, draw-ers and drawer tracks were made entirely of wood.

This early drawer style is used when building rustic or country pine furniture, and, if accurately assembled, is still very functional.

Build the drawer box so it's ⅛" narrower than the opening and ⅛" less in height. The drawer face is normally ½" wide and taller than the opening.

The drawing below details the joinery for a drawer opening that's 8"x17¼"x18".

All material is ¾" thick except the ¼" bottom board.

Materials List		
No.	Item	Dimensions T W L
2	Sides	¾"x7⅞"x17"
1	Front	¾"x7⅞"x16⅞"
1	Back	¾"x7⅛"x16⅞"
1	Bottom	¼"x16½"x16⅞"
2	Drawer front	¾"x8½"x18½"

Cut all the drawer parts. The front side boards require a ¼"-wide by ¼"-deep dado that begins ½" up from the bottom edges. Attach the sides to the back and front board with glue and finishing nails.

Slide the ¼" plywood bottom into the dadoes. It should fit snug in the side board dadoes and go all the way into the front dado. It should cover the back board edge completely. Nail the bottom board to the back board edge. Do not use glue.

Install the drawer box in the cabinet. Round over the front edges of the drawer face, and secure it in place. It should over-lap the opening by ¼" on all edges. Attach the face with four 1¼" screws through the inside of the drawer box.

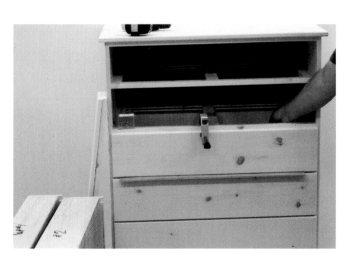

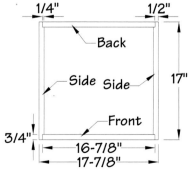

The drawer assembly.

Toy Storage Center

Paul Hill, a cabinetmaker who lives near me, developed this toy-storage project idea. He was tired of stepping on the children's building blocks and toy soldiers and decided to find a solution.

His answer was this toy storage center. Hopefully, there would be no more stepping on all those action figures and other small toys.

I've chosen pine to match the children's bedroom furniture. However, you can build it from any wood, including inexpensive plywood should you wish to keep this project in the basement.

A few people who have seen the completed project thought it would be useful as a sewing-goods storage center or a food bin in a cold room. I'm sure there are many other potential applications.

Be sure to buy the plastic bins before starting the project. You may have to alter the dimensions slightly, depending on the container sizes you use.

Rubbermaid manufactured the bins I used. They were 3 U.S. gal/11.3 l models. Product # JLO-222o-CO HGRN.

Materials List

All material is ¾"-thick pine with the exception of a ¼" plywood back board.

No.	Item	Dimensions T W L
2	Sides	¾"x17"x30"
2	Vertical partitions	¾"x16¾"x30"
1	Base board	¾"x17"x37⅞"
1	Top	¾"x18"x39⅞"
24	Cleats	¾"x¾"x16¾"
1	Back board	¼"x30½"x36⅞"
2	Base frame boards	¾"x2"x33⅞"
2	Base frame boards	¾"x2"x11½"

BUILDING THE STORAGE CENTER

Step 1. Make the Panels

Glue up enough material to make two sides, two partitions, one top and one bottom panel. See page 126 for instructions on creating solid wood panels.

Cut them to size, as detailed in the materials list.

Step 2. Prepare the Panels

Before assembly begins, cut dadoes and rabbets in the top and bottom panel.

First, the bottom panel has a ¼"-thick by ¼"-deep rabbet that is stopped ½" short of each end. This rabbet is on the bottom board's rear top face.

Second, the top board also has a ¼"-thick by ¼"-deep rabbet, stopped 1½" from each end, on its rear underside.

Next, cut a ¼"-thick by ¼"-deep rabbet on each side board. This joint is on the inside back face of the side panel. These rabbets will accept the back board.

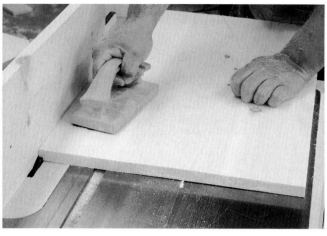

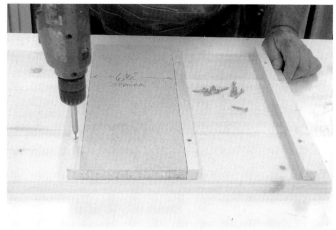

Step 2. Cut rabbet and dado joints on a table saw with a dado blade.   **Step 3.** Use a 6½"-wide spacer board, and install the wood cleats.

Step 3. Install the Cleats

Attach the cleats to the sides and partitions as shown in the drawing. Use glue and screws. Start the first cleat 1" down from the top. Using a spacer board cut to 6½" wide, install the remainder of the cleats.

Step 4. Attach the Bottom Board

Attach the sides to the bottom board so they are flush with the ends. Cut an 11⅝" spacer, and attach the partitions.

Secure the sides and partitions from the underside of the bottom board with 2" screws. Apply glue to the ends of the boards before securing them in place.

Step 5. Install the Top

Using the same 11⅝" spacer board, attach the top to the ends of the sides and partition panels.

The top board overhangs each side panel by 1" and the front edges of the vertical panels by the same amount.

Step 6. Attach the Back Board

Use a ¼" veneer plywood that matches the solid wood for the back board.

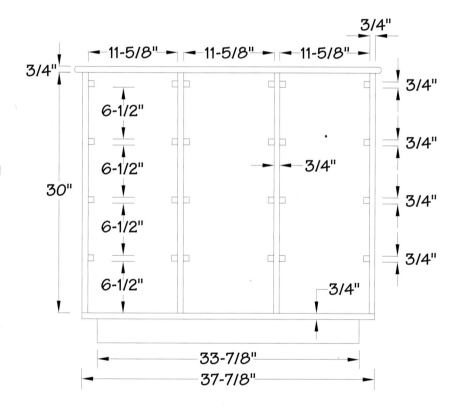

The toy storage center.

Use glue and brad nails to attach the back in the rabbet joints cut in the side, top and bottom boards.

Step 7. Construct the Base Frame

Build a base frame with an outside measurement of 2"x13"x33⅝".

Attach it to the base board with glue and screws installed from the top side of the bottom board. Plug the counterbored screw holes, and final sand the cabinet.

Step 4. Attach the side and partition boards to the bottom board.

Step 5. Attach the top to the sides and partition panels. Use 2" wood screws in counterbored holes that will have wood plugs installed. Use glue and three screws per panel. Always predrill the screw hole.

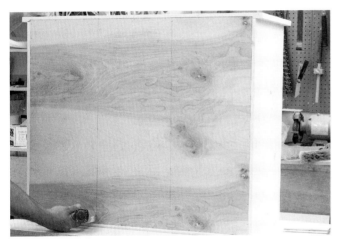

Step 6. The ¼"-thick back board rests in the rabbets and is secured with glue and brad nails.

Step 7. Install the base, and sand the cabinet. Test fit the plastic bins, and apply a finish. I used three coats of oil-based polyurethane.

Special Storage

Completed Murphy-style fold-down bed project.

Murphy-Style Fold-Down Bed Options

Once upon a time, building a Murphy-style fold-down bed was an intimidating project. Today, however, there's a simple mechanism available that makes the project much easier.

I built a Murphy-style fold-down bed many years ago. It served a useful purpose, but it was heavy to operate. Two adults were needed to raise and lower the bed. I was never comfortable with the project.

My design was based on the use of a 1½"-diameter pipe. It was the pivot and headboard end support for the bed. In the top left photo on page 137, you can see the pipe running through the bed frame and its support points in each bookcase.

The top right photo on page 137 shows the bed in the "down" position, resting on the pipe at the headboard end and a set of fold-down legs at the footboard end.

I discovered a company called Create-A-Bed that was marketing a fold-down bed mechanism that had been in use in the hotel industry. They have now released it for sale to the home market.

I checked out a few different design options and returned to this hardware. The kit includes a set of pistons that control the speed of

My first Murphy-style fold-down bed project was supported with a 1½" pipe as the pivot.

The bed was heavy to operate and required two adults to raise and lower the bed frame.

PHOTO: Create-A-Bed Inc.

This Murphy-style fold-down bed is hidden away in a box.

PHOTO: Create-A-Bed Inc.

When opened, the bed appears to be a "normal" bed and is ready for your guests.

the bed as it's raised or lowered.

The pivot hardware on the modern kits is a double plate with a heavy steel pin. One plate is attached to the bed frame, the other is fixed on the upright support.

In the lower right photo on page 138, the plate at the head of the bed is used to attach the piston assembly to the movable frame.

Building the Bed Platform

The mattress platform is a straightforward woodworking project. A frame similar to the platform bed project (page 113) or the children's storage bed (page 128) can be used.

A word of caution before you begin the construction: Hardware kits, such as the one from Create-A-Bed, have set sequences of building procedures because of the special assembly requirements with the hardware.

It's also interesting to note that this manufacturer supplies complete drawings for the platform and part of the cabinet for vertical and horizontal fold-down models.

Door Options

The fold-down bed system needs large doors. They can be simple slab doors (see the laundry room project in chapter four), or they can have additional design features (see the tall cabinets in chapter seven).

In fact, the towers that were used in chapter seven can be the side cabinets for the fold-down bed.

With the commercially available kits, the "doors" are actually part of the drop-down platform for the mattress. In some cases, the feet at the footboard end are hinged on the platform and look like handles.

Cabinet Styles

The cabinets on either side of the fold-down bed mechanism can be simple bookcases. Doors can be attached to the lower portion of the case and for hidden storage. The cabinets at each side can be as wide as you desire. They are limited only by the amount of space you have available.

Murphy-style fold-down beds can be concealed in fancy wall systems that provide more storage space for books and collectibles.

PHOTO: Create-A-Bed Inc.

PHOTO: Create-A-Bed Inc.

The bottoms of these Murphy-style fold-down beds are also the cabinet doors. In this unit, the doors are treated with an applied molding, which adds interest to the cabinet. The "handles" on the doors are hinged and become bed legs when the unit is opened.

The piston mechanism controls the bed-swing speed during opening and closing.

The fold-down bed pivots on a pin and bushing that is mounted on the bed frame and fixed upright support.

The Basic Bookcase

A bookcase can be used in any room and doesn't have to be fancy. It's often hidden by books, collectibles or other family treasures. Here's a simple alternative for building this useful storage project.

BUILDING THE BOOKCASE

Step 1. Prepare the Sides, Top and Bottom

Cut the sides, top and bottom boards. Router a dado for the ¼" back on the inside back of the side boards, top back of the bottom board, and bottom back of the top board. This rabbet will be ¼"-deep by ¼"-wide.

Step 2. Drill Shelf Pin Holes

Drill two columns of ½"-diameter holes, spaced 4" apart, on the inside of each side board.

Step 3. Join the Boards

Attach the top and bottom boards to the sides with glue and screws. Insert the screws from the outside face of the side boards, and fill the holes with wood plugs.

The completed bookcase project.

NO-ROUTER OPTION

If you don't have access to a router, apply the ¼" back board on the edge of the top, bottom and side boards. The shelf boards can then be left at 7¼" deep. Increase the back board to 37½"-wide by 80"-high.

Materials List

All material is ¾"-thick solid pine with the exception of the back board.

No.	Item	Dimensions T W L
2	Sides	¾"x7¼"x84"
1	Top	¾"x7¼"x36"
1	Bottom	¾"x7¼"x36"
1	Back	¼"x36½"x79"
2	Stiles	¾"x1½"x84"
2	Rails	¾"x4¾"x34½"
6	Shelves	¾"x7"x35⅞"
24	Shelf pins	½" diameter x 1½" long

Step 2. Drill two columns of holes in each side board ½" in diameter and ½" deep. Space the holes at 4" centers.

Step 3. Attach the top board flush with the side's top edges. The bottom board, or fixed shelf, is installed so its top edge is 4¾" up from the bottom of the side boards.

Step 5. The stiles (vertical members) are attached to the bookcase with glue and finishing nails.

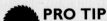

PRO TIP

Try to cut the back as accurately as possible. If the back is cut properly, it will hold the corners square, thus making the cabinet square.

The top board is flush with the top edge of the sides. The bottom board's top surface is 4¾" up from the side board's bottom edge.

Step 4. Install the Back Board

Secure the back in the rabbets with glue and brad nails. If you are using the "no-router" option, attach it to the back edges of the top, bottom and side boards with glue and brad nails.

Step 5. Attach the Stiles

Cut two stiles and attach them to the edges of the side boards. The outside edges of the stiles should be flush with the outside faces of the side boards.

Use glue and finishing nails. The nail holes can be filled with wood putty to match the final finish applied to the bookcase.

Step 6. The Rails

The rails can be straight or with an arc cut on their bottom edges. This feature softens the look of a large bookcase.

A simple arc template can be made using a thin piece of wood. Bend the thin piece in an arc, and clamp it 2" in from each end of the rail. Mark the arc with a pencil, and cut out the template with a jigsaw. Sand the cut smooth, and use it as a template for the top and bottom rails.

Step 7. Install the Rails

Attach the top and bottom rail with glue and nails. Use 2" screws through the stile edges into the rails. One per joint is adequate. Fill the nail holes with wood putty and the screw holes with wood plugs.

Step 6. Create a template for the rails. Cut both arcs and sand them smooth.

Step 7. Install the upper and lower rails with glue and nails into the top and bottom board edges. Draw the rails tight to the stiles with a screw through the stile edge into the rail end.

Step 9. Make as many shelf pins from the ½"-diameter dowel rod as required.

Step 8. Rounding over the edges of the stiles and rails softens the appearance of this large bookcase.

Step 8. Soften the Edges

Round over all the edges of the stiles and rails with a ¼" router bit.

Step 9. Add Adjustable Shelves

Cut 1½" lengths of ½" dowel rod. You will need four times the number of shelves that will be used. Push the shelf pins into the holes and install the shelves.

This basic bookcase can be made from any wood you desire. For the basement, inexpensive plywood or any other board that can be painted is perfectly acceptable.

You can also build the case from knotty pine, to match the furniture in chapter nine, or possibly oak, to match the bedroom or family room projects in this book.

SOURCES

The following suppliers' products were used in the production of projects for this book. They were supportive in supplying materials and information. I would like to thank them for their time and efforts in helping to make this book possible.

Black & Decker
Hampstead, MD
800-345-3947
http://www.blackanddecker.com
Woodworking tools.

Create-A-Bed, Inc.
Louisville, KY
502-966-3852
http://www.wallbed.com
Create-A-Bed wall bed
    hardware.

House of Tools
Edmonton, Alberta
800-661-3987
Woodworking tools and supplies.

Jesada Tools
Oldsmar, FL
800-531-5559
http://jesada.com
Woodworking tools.

JessEm Tool Co.
Penetanguishene, Ontario
800-436-6799
http://www.jessem.com
Manufacturer of the Rout-R-Slide
    router table.

Porter-Cable
Jackson, TN
901-668-8600
http://www.porter-cable.com
Woodworking tools.

Richelieu Hardware
Dorval, Quebec
800-361-6000
http://www.richelieu.com
Cabinetmaking hardware supply to
    professional cabinetmakers.

Tenryu America, Inc.
Melbourne, FL
800-451-7297
http://www.tenryu.com
Makers of high quality saw blades.

**Rockler Woodworking &
    Hardware**
Medina, MN
800-279-4441
http://www.rockler.com
Woodworking tools and supplies.

Tool Trend
Concord, Ontario
800-387-7005
http://tooltrend.com/canada
Woodworking tools and supplies.

White Home Products
Thomasville, GA
800-200-9272
http://closets.net
Closet storage systems and accessories.

Wolfcraft, Inc.
Itasca, IL
630-773-4777
http://www.wolfcraft.com
Woodworking tools.

Woodcraft Supply Corp.
Parkersburg, WV
800-535-4482
http://www.woodcraft.com
Woodworking hardware.

Woodworker's Hardware
Sauk Rapids, MN
800-383-0130
Woodworking hardware.

INDEX

INDEX